THIS NOTEBOOK BELONGS TO

DATE STARTED

DATE FINISHED

练习纸

MW00903649

CHINESE PRACTICE PAPER NOTEBOOKS
HANZI GRIDS

练习纸

STARTING OUT

SKILL LEVEL

MORE ADVANCED

九宫格 Jiu Gong Ge Paper
nine-palace practice paper

Ideal for those just starting out. Features 3x3 grid to help guide vertical and horizontal lines.

米字格 Mi Zi Ge Paper
RICE-STYLE PRACTICE PAPER

The preferred practice paper of Chinese native speakers and calligraphers. Features rice style gride lines to help develop perfectly proportioned characters.

田字格 Tian Zi Ge Paper
FIELD-STYLE Practice paper

Features 2x2 field-style grid guile lines for writing Chinese characters, especially characters that depend on symmetry to be legible.

拼音田字格 Pinyin Tian Zi Ge Paper
PINYIN & FIELD-STYLE practice paper

Features the same Field-Grid as Tian Zi Ge Paper, but with space above the Field-Grid for writing Hanyu Pinyin characters. Useful for practicing pinyin-character pairs.

拼音格 Pinyin Paper
HANYU PINYIN Practice paper

Ideal for practicing Hanyu Pinyin characters. Features row grid guide lines.

回宫格 Hui Gong Ge Paper
Palace practice paper

Improve your penmanship by using Hui Gong Ge Paper to develop better aligned characters.

方字格 Fang Zi Ge Paper
SQUARE-GRID practice paper

Ideal for those ready to practice writing Chinese characters without guiding grid lines. This versatile paper facilitates practice using any number of styles.

短文格 Essay Paper
HOMEWORK / ESSAY Paper

Perfect for homework and essays. Each page features a 20x20 (400 Square) Hanzi grid with space between rows for student notes/thoughts.

Also Available From Grumpy Robot Journals: Korean & Japanese Practice Paper

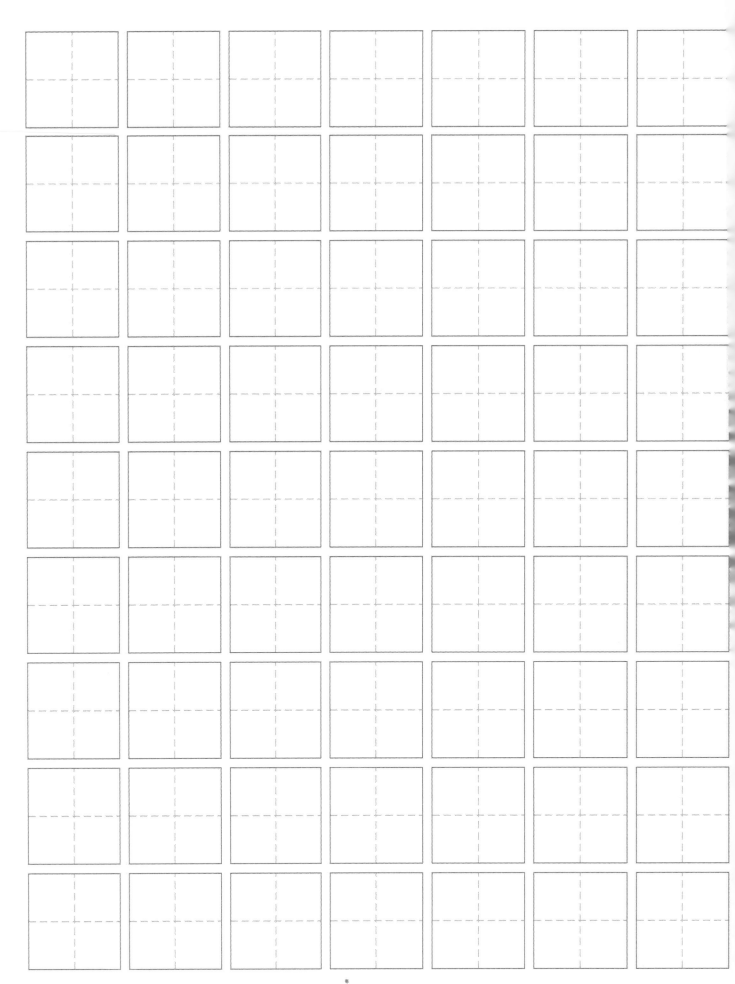

曉機器人

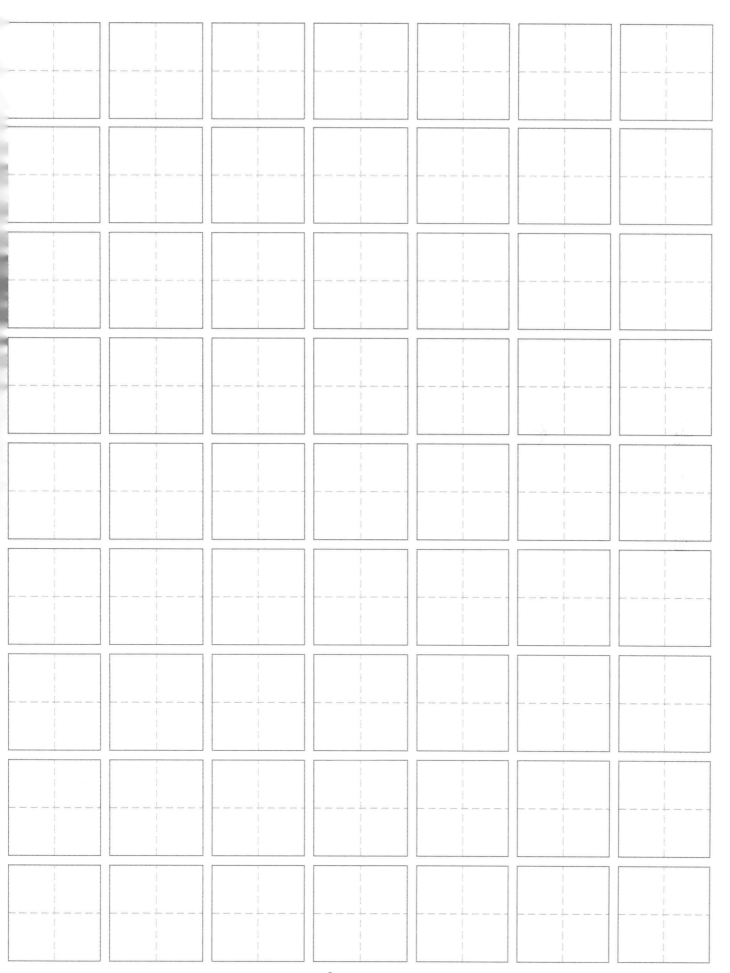

曉機器人

曉機器人

曉機器人

嘵機器人

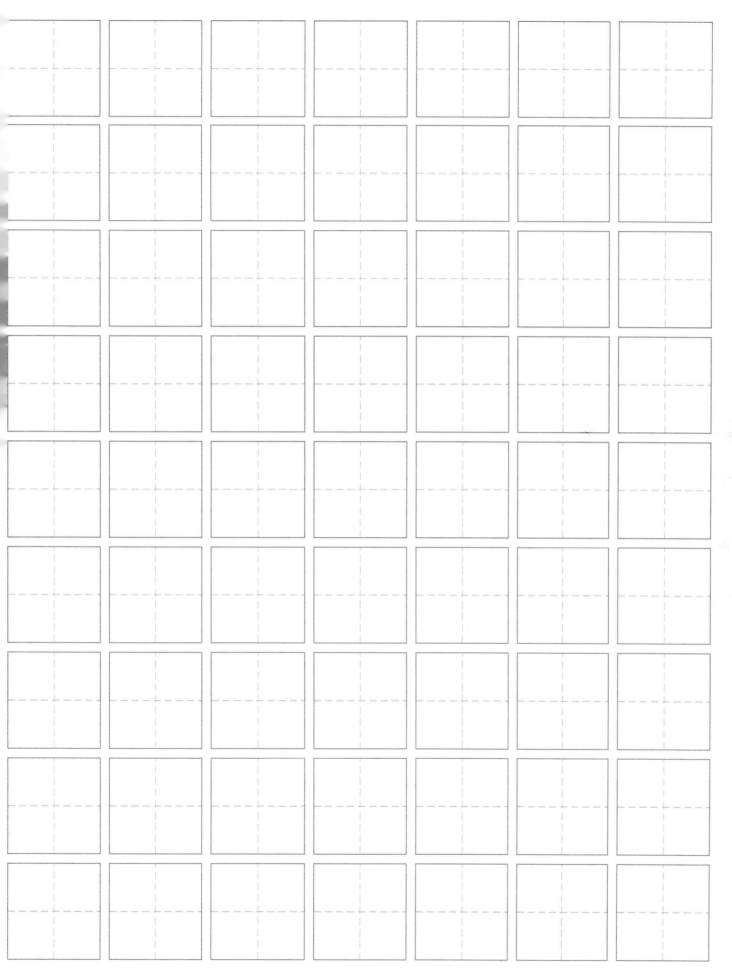

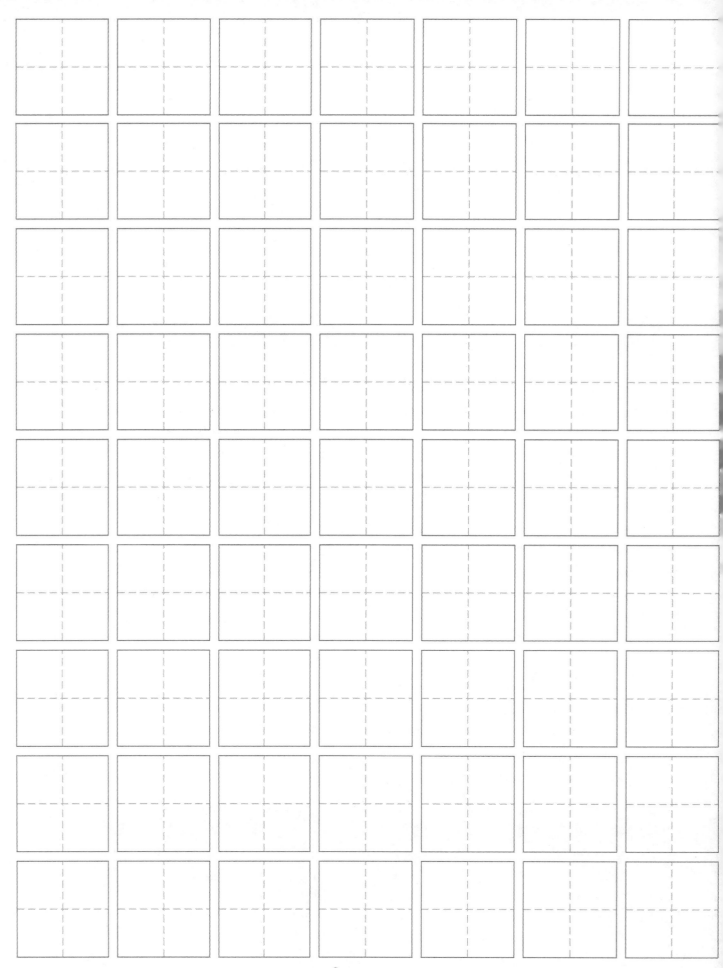

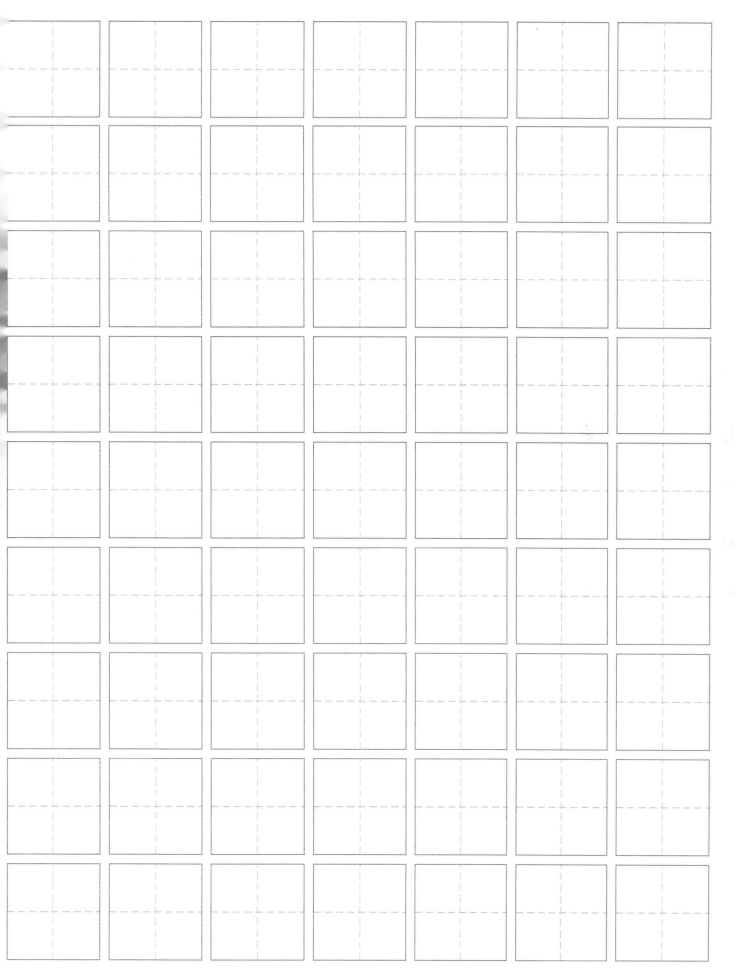

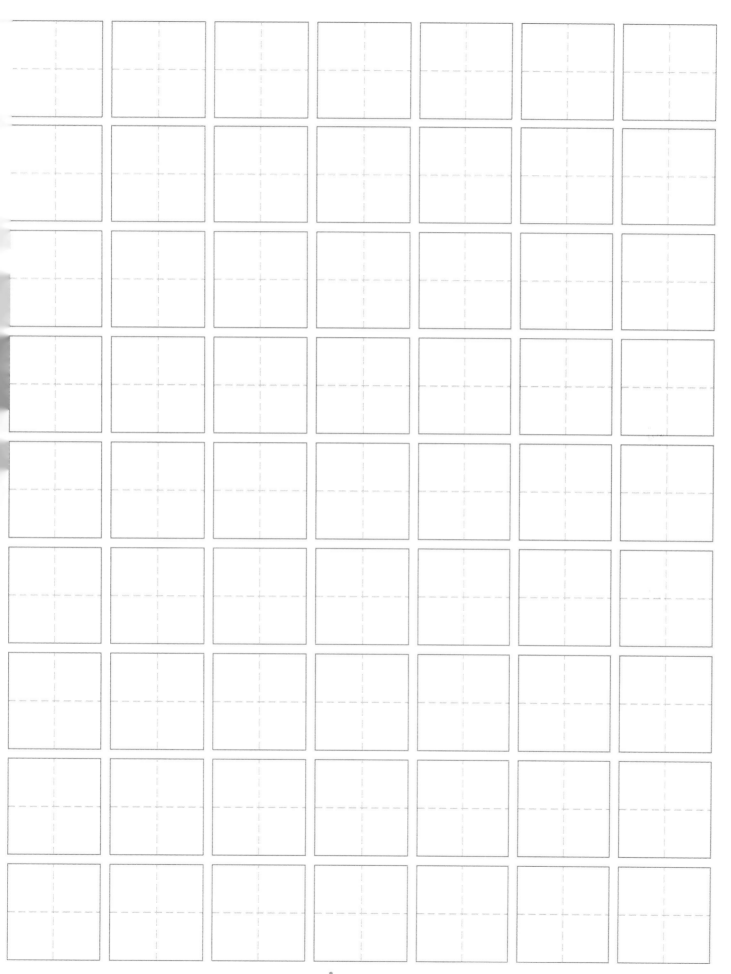

曉機器人

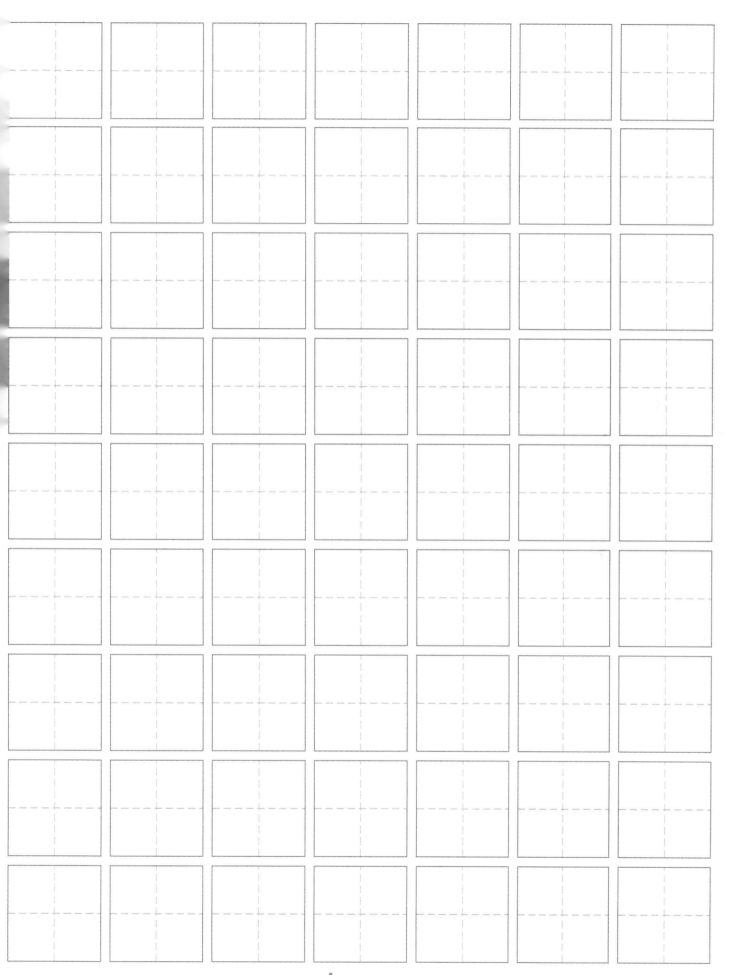

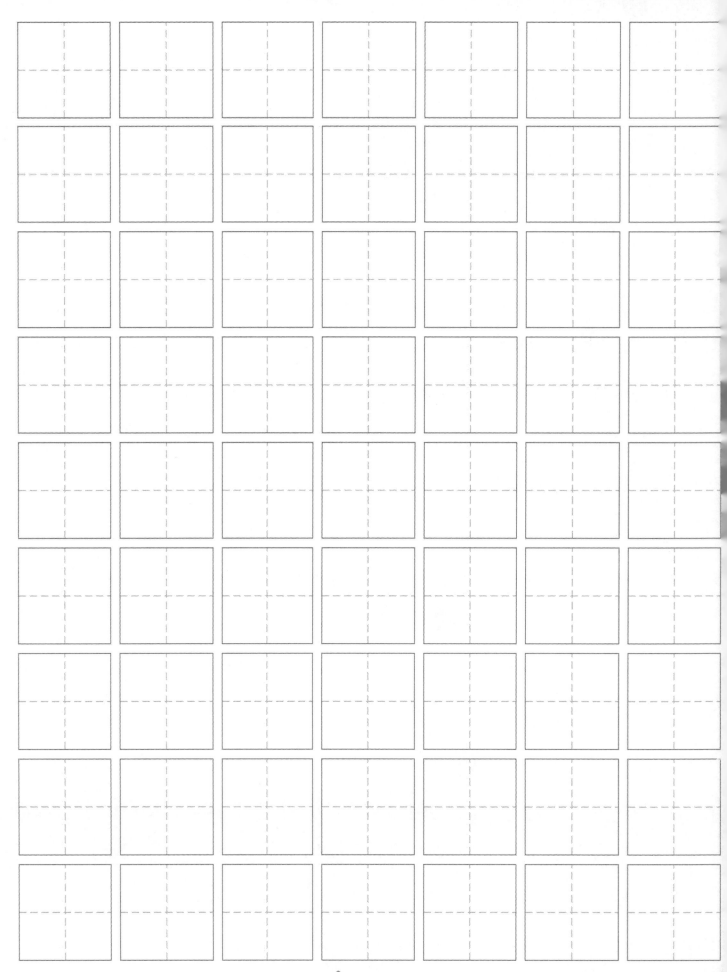

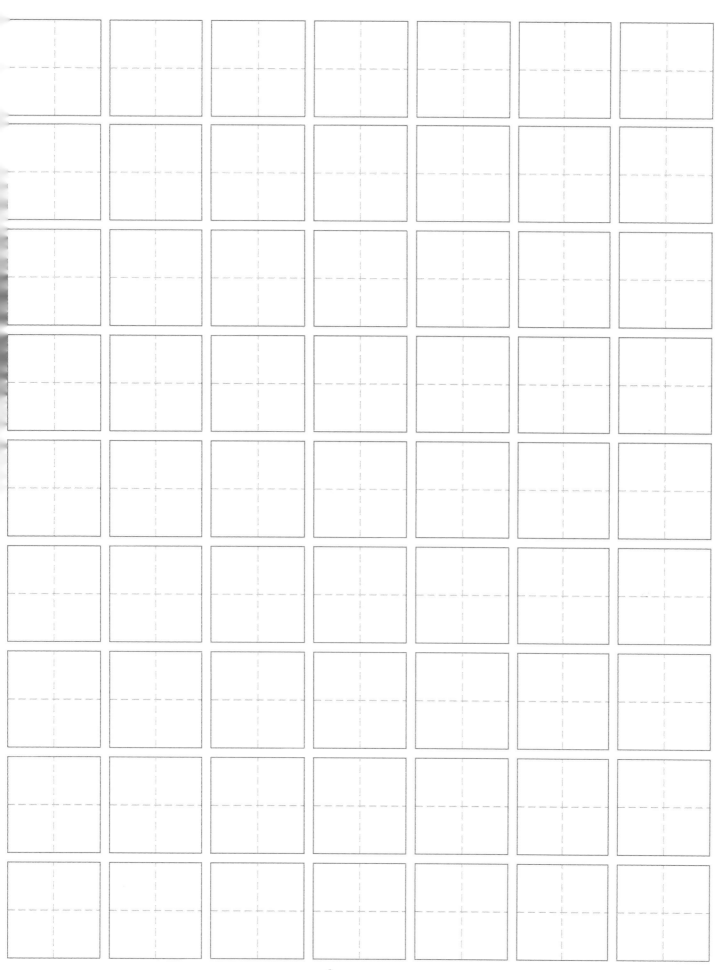

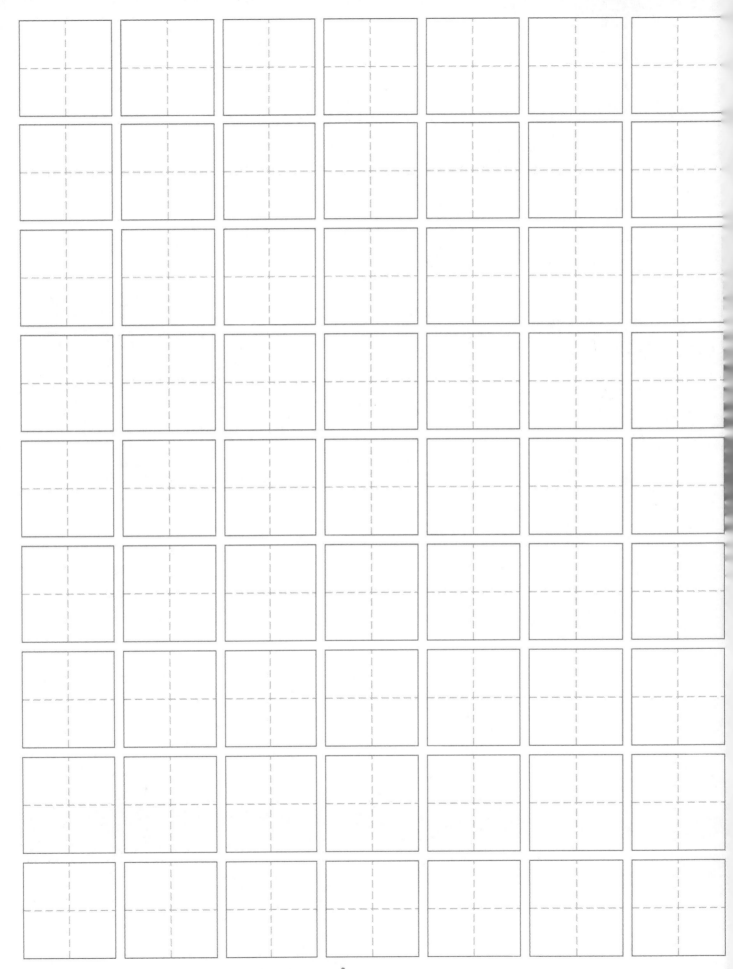

曉機器人

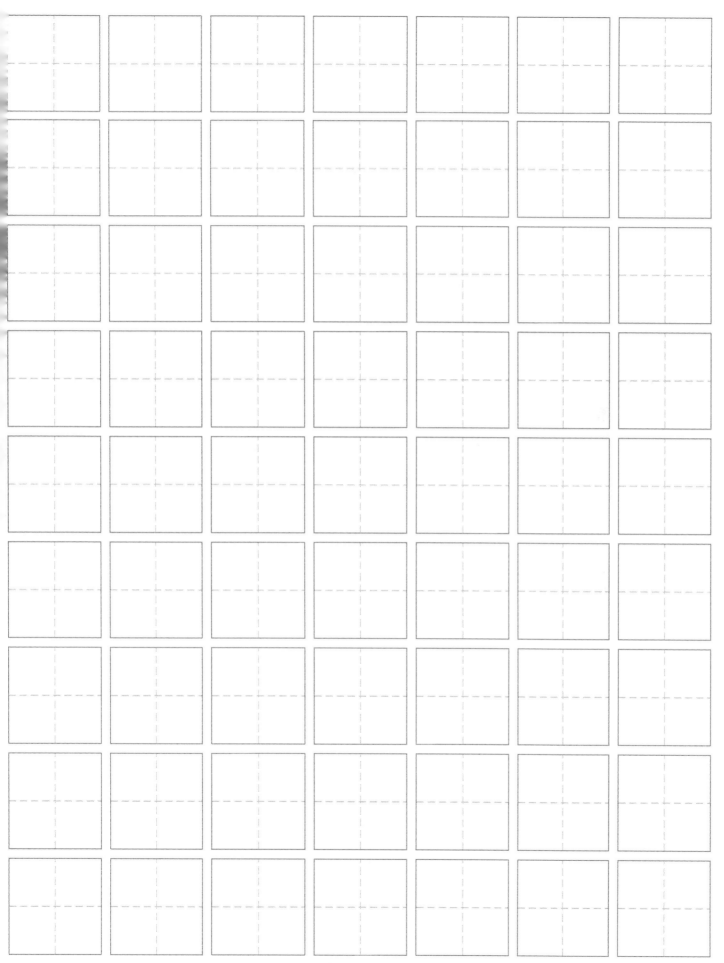

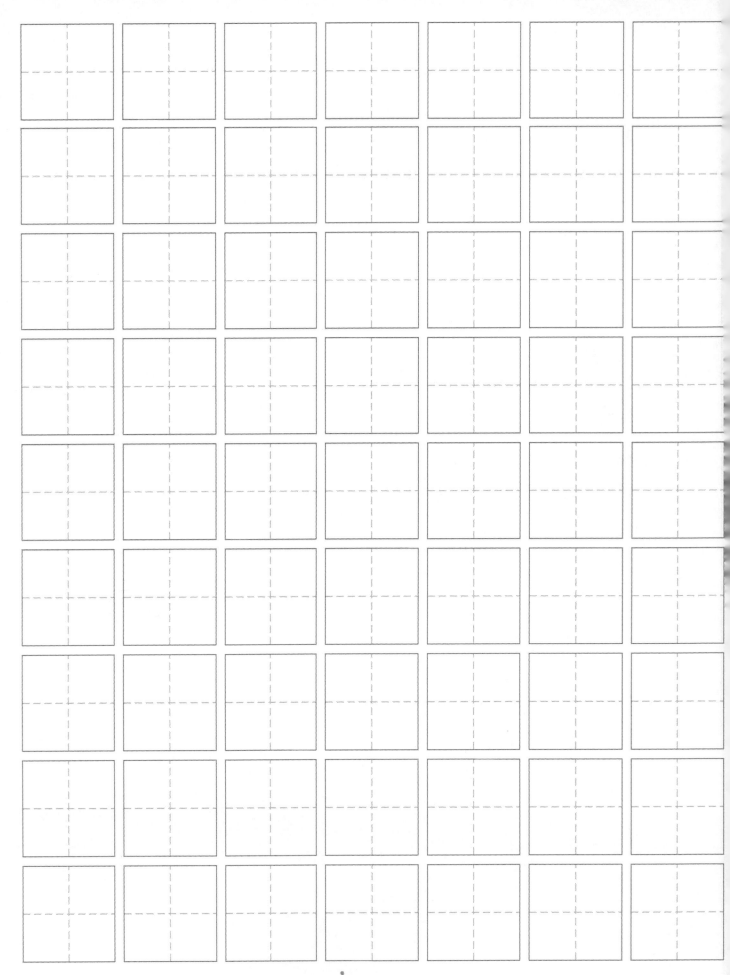

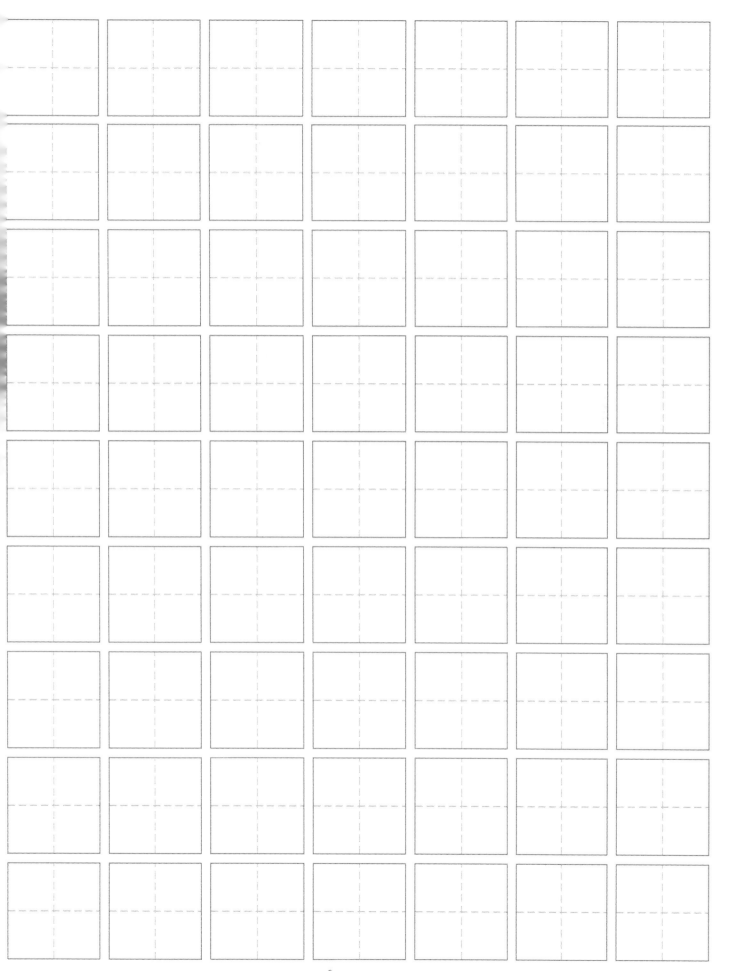

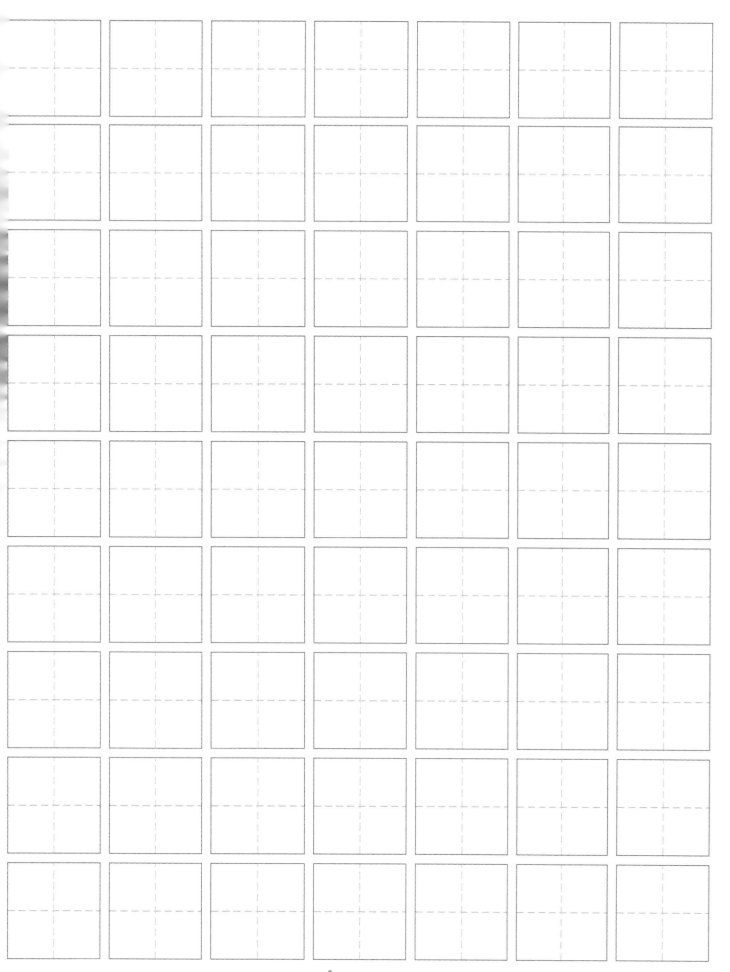

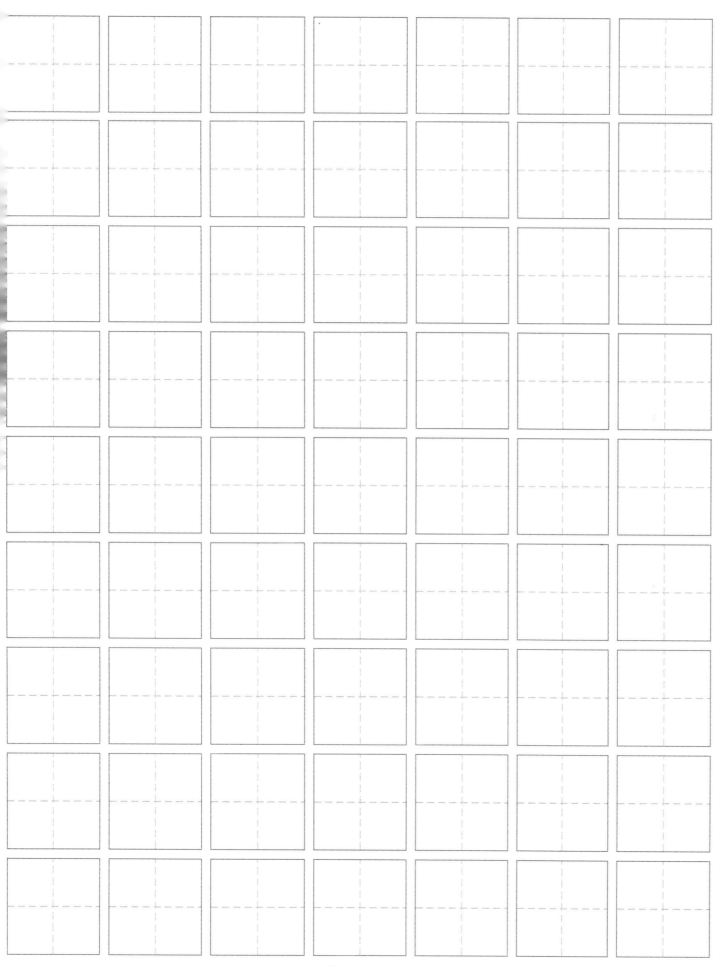

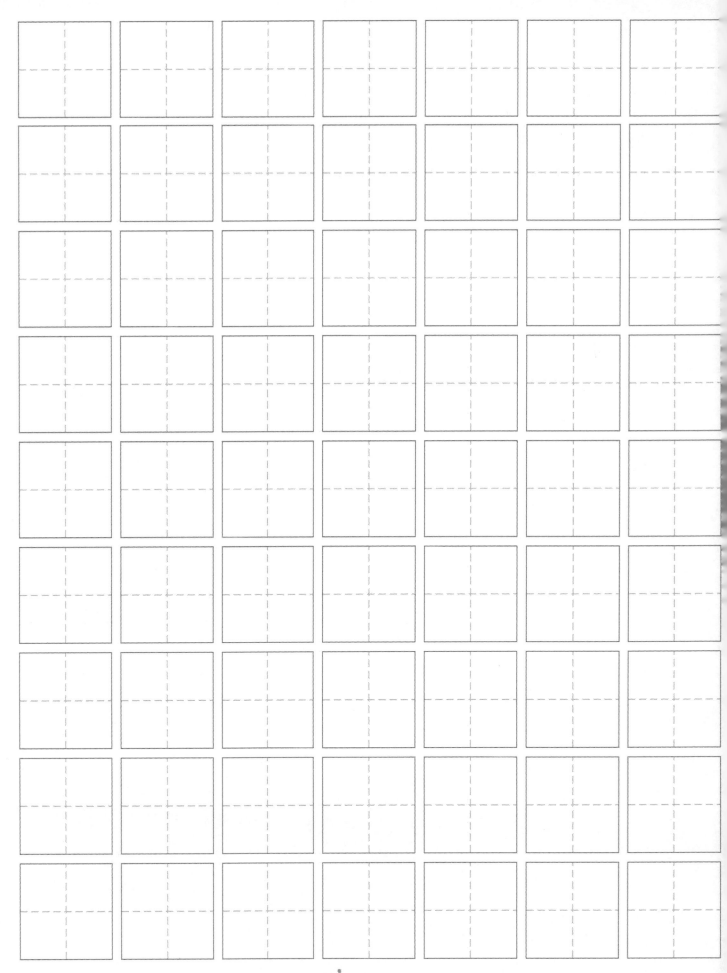

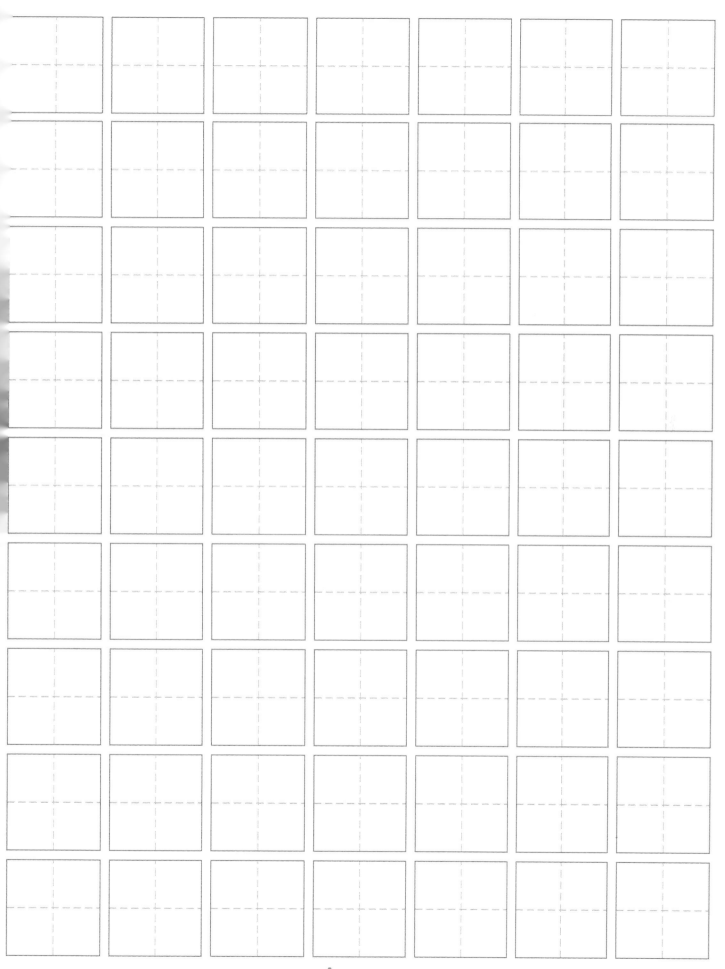

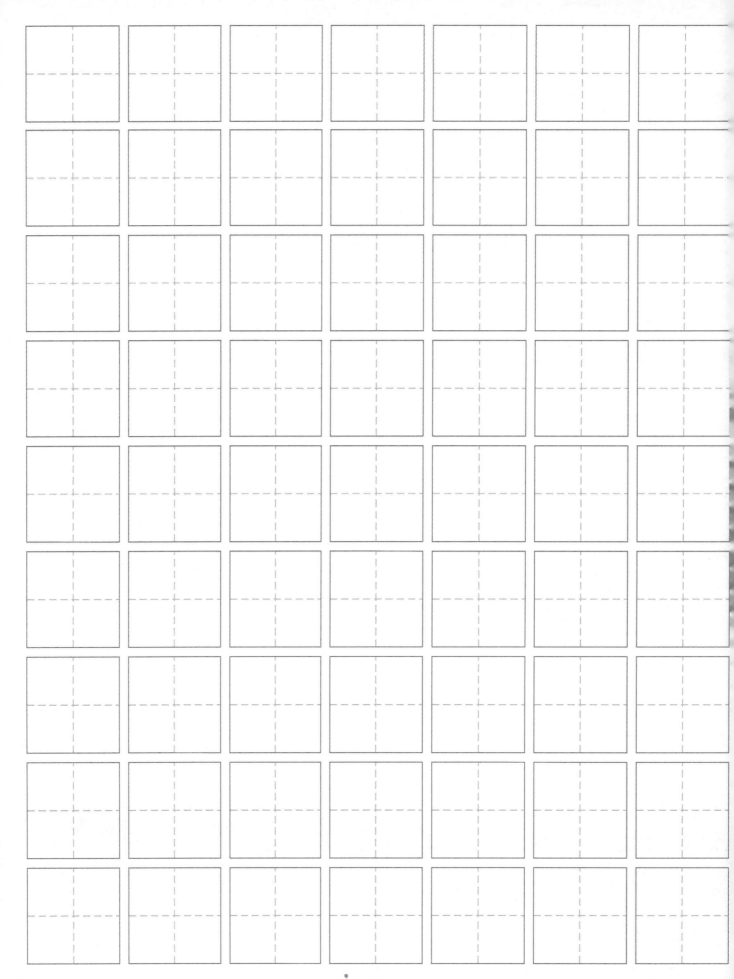

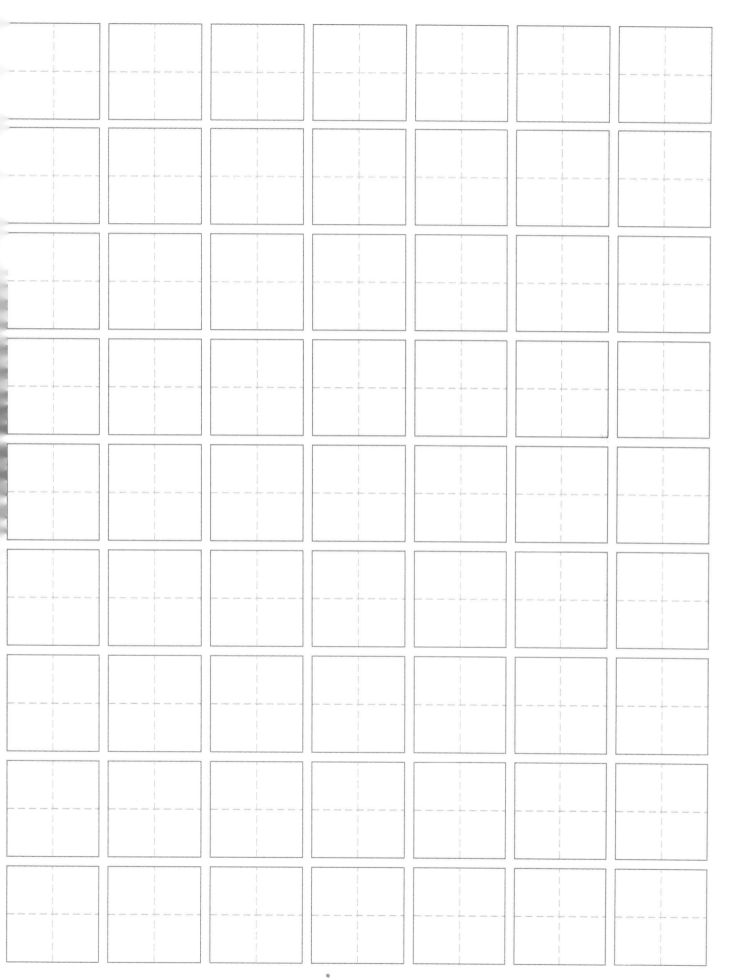

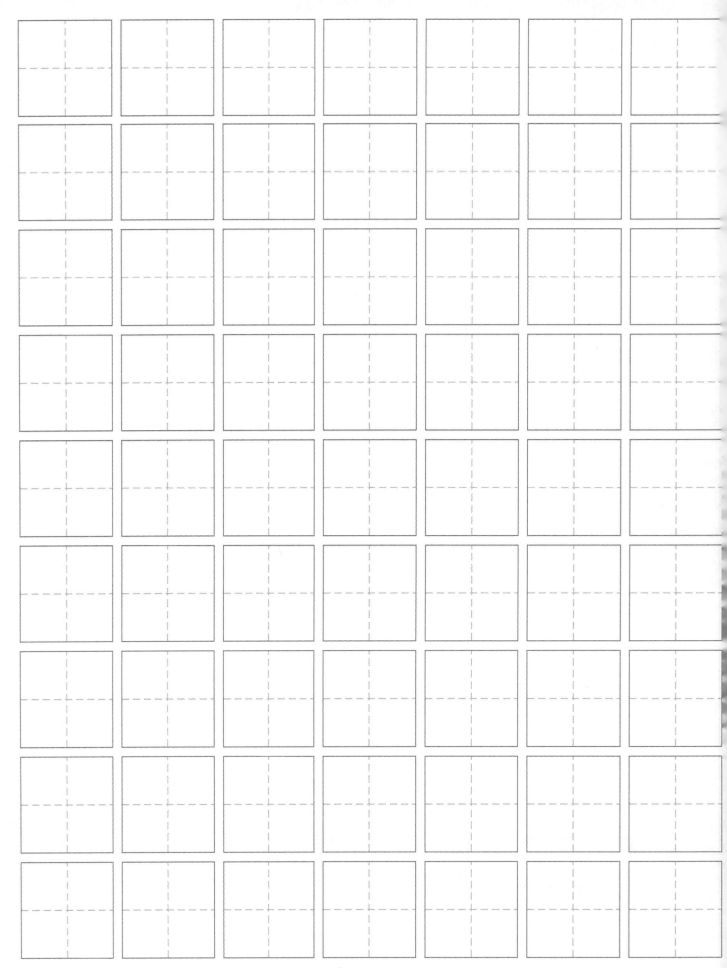

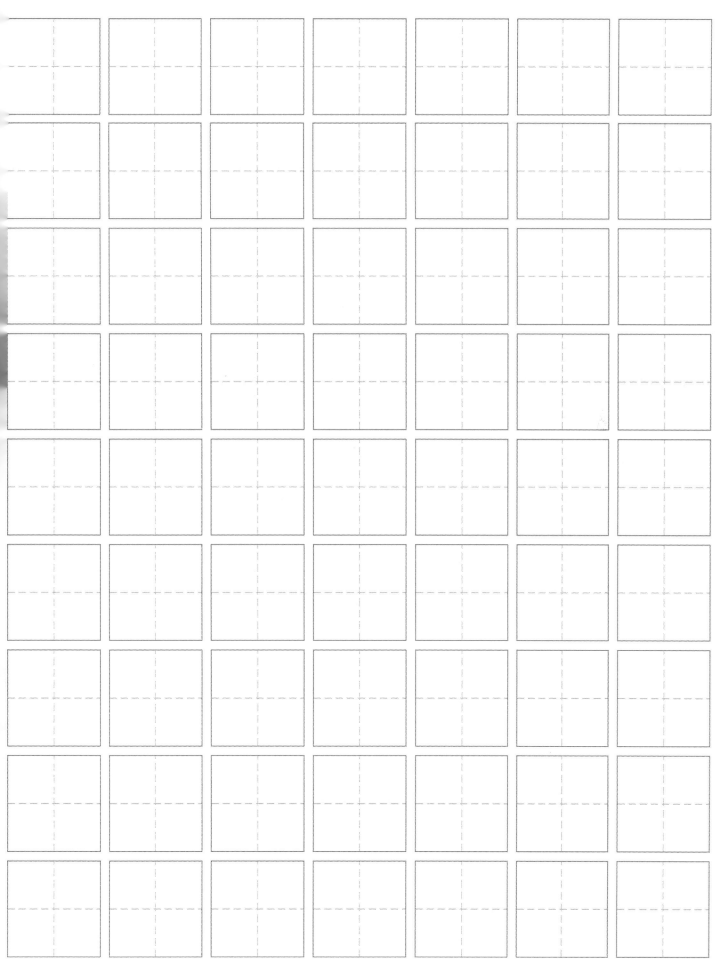

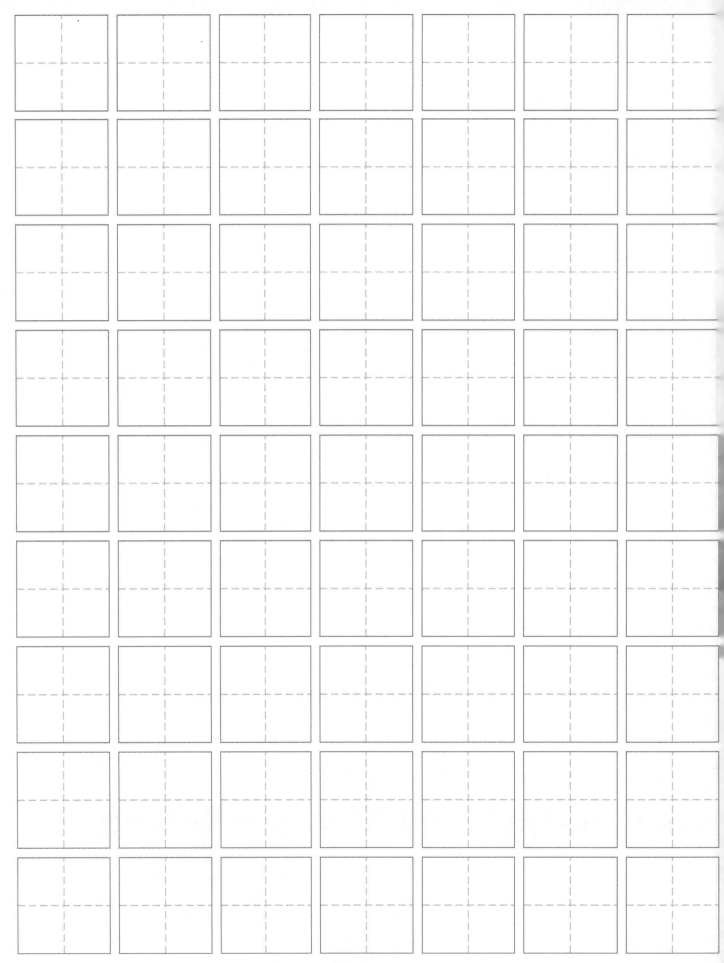

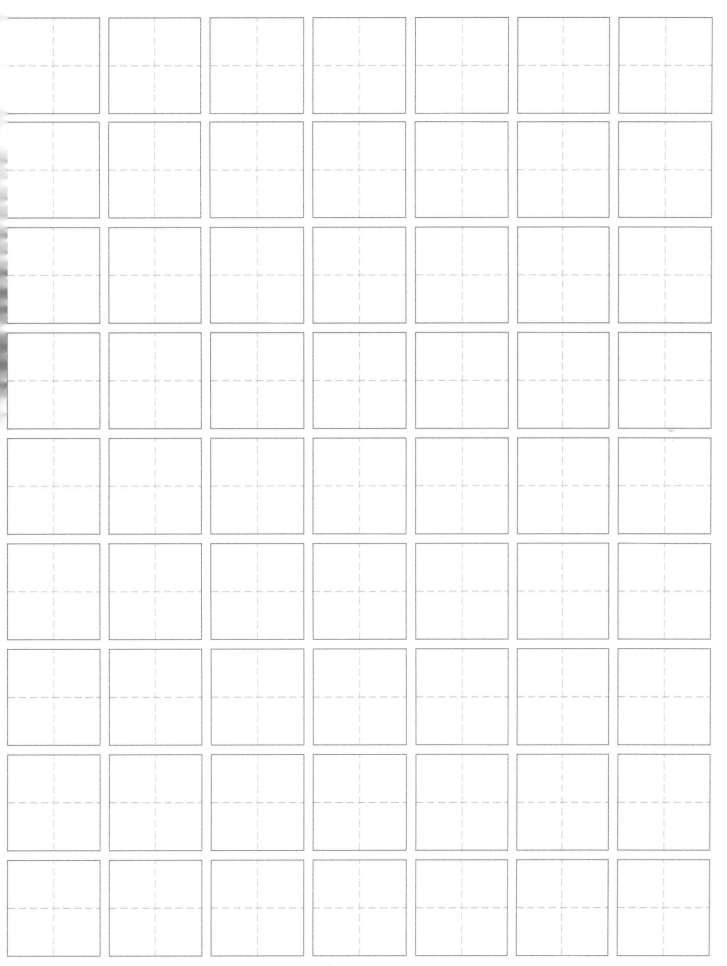

曉機器人

曉機器人

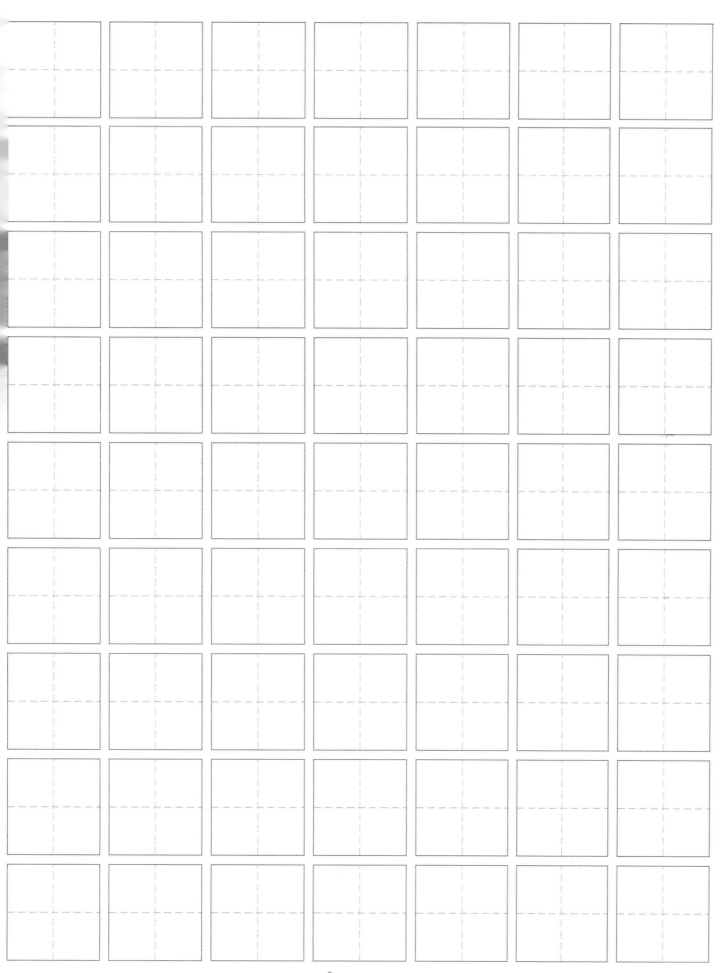

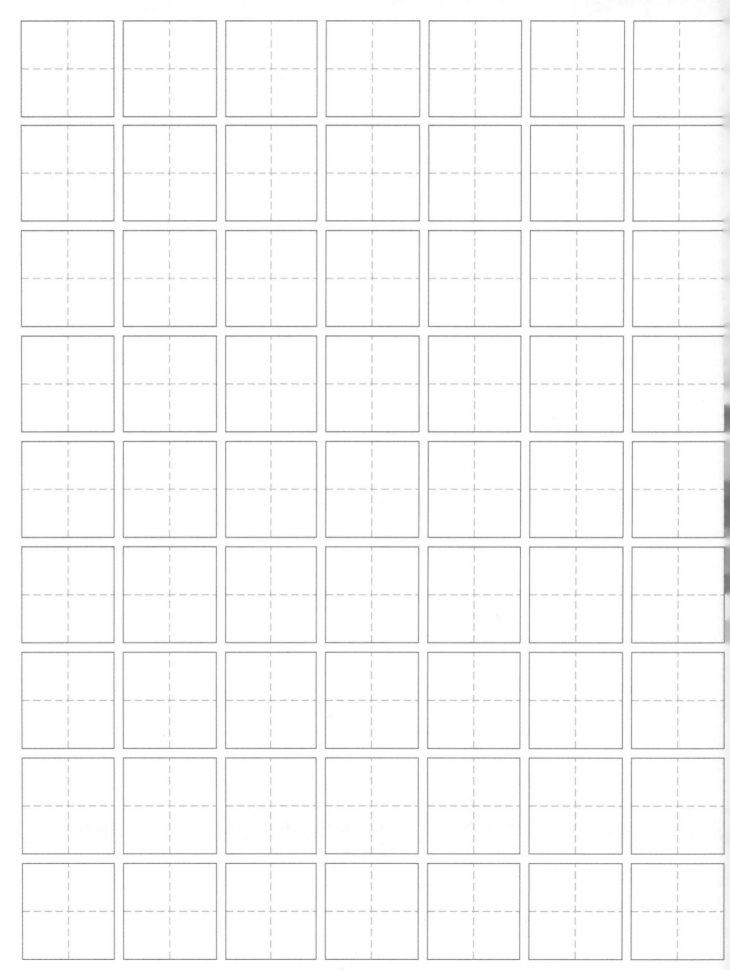

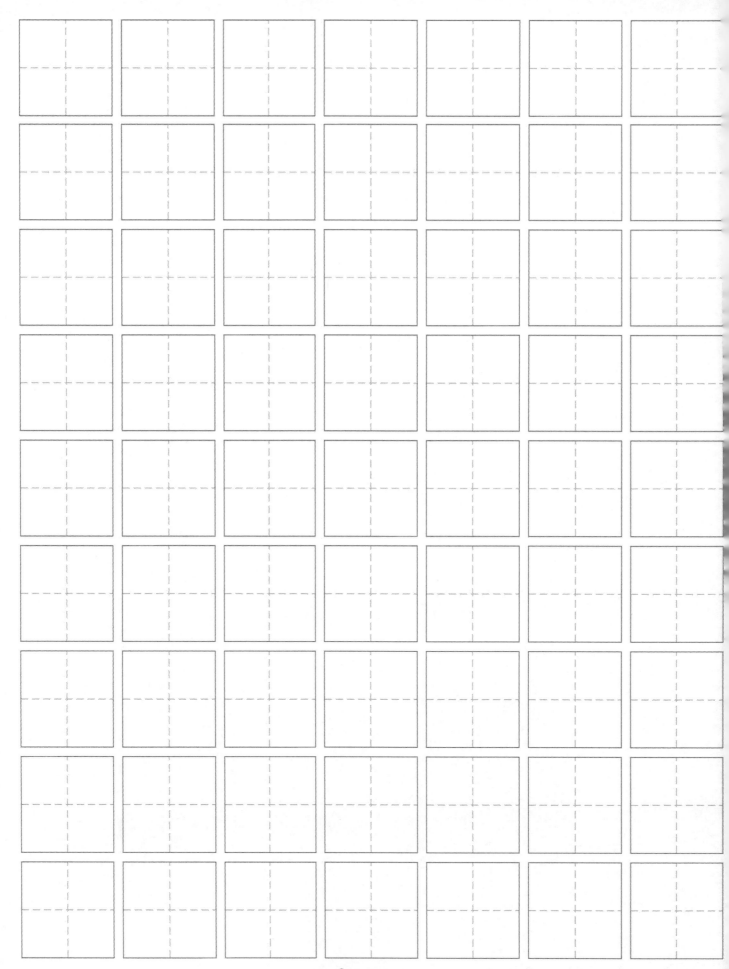

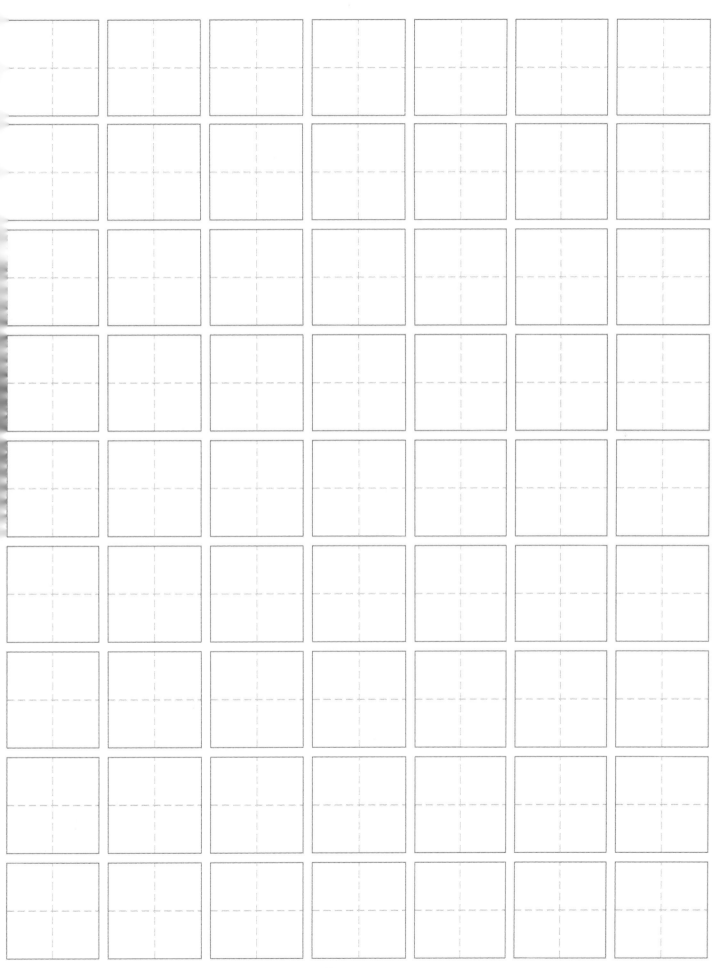

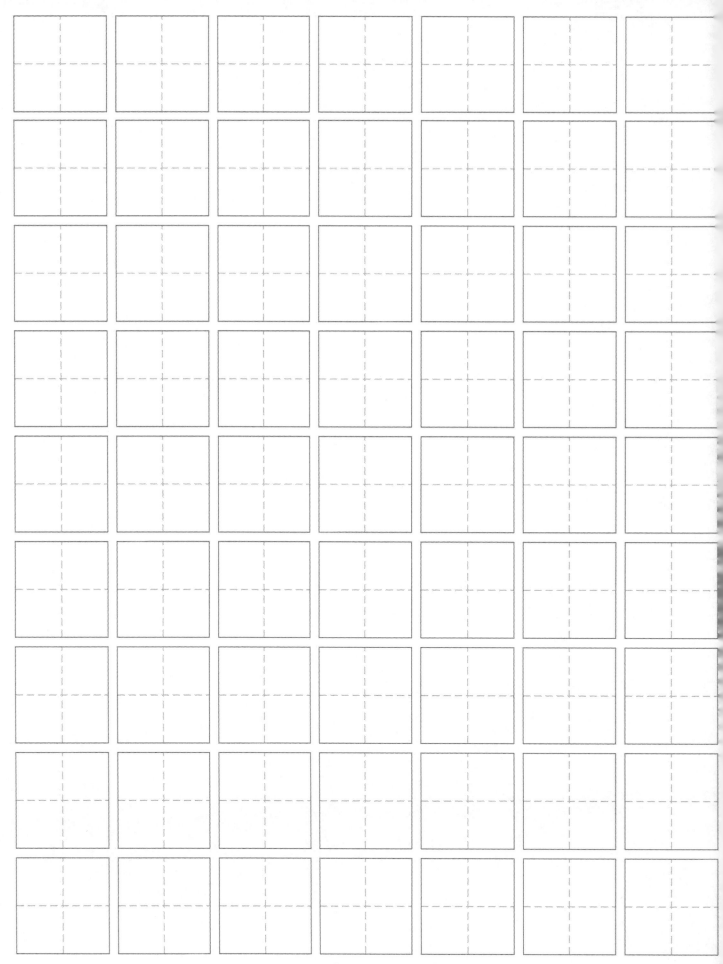

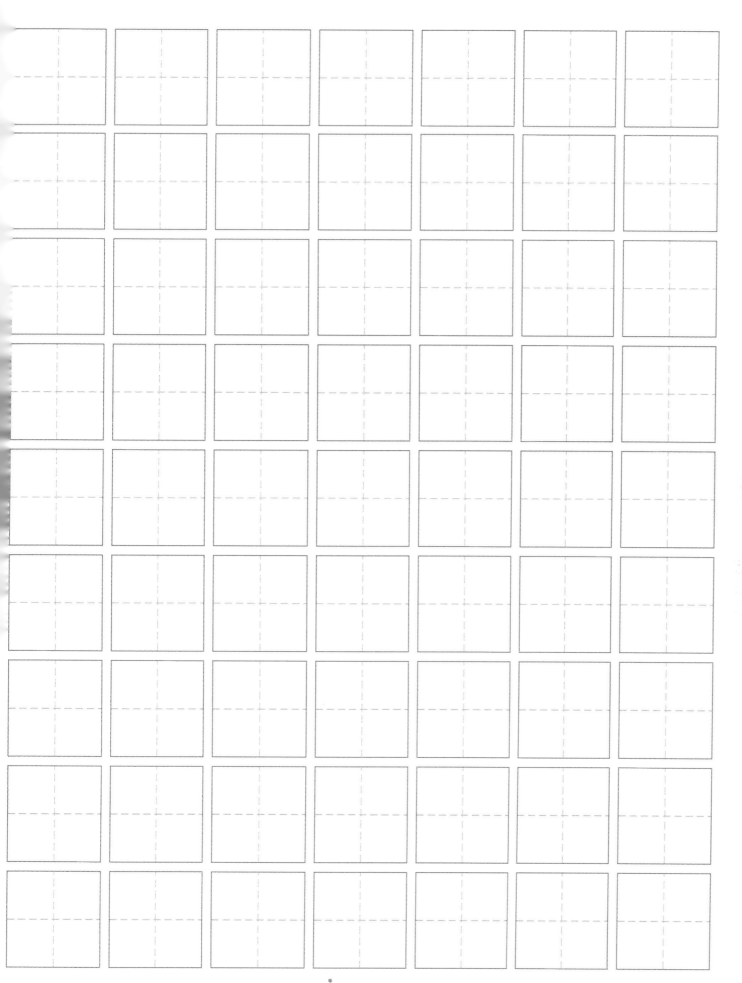

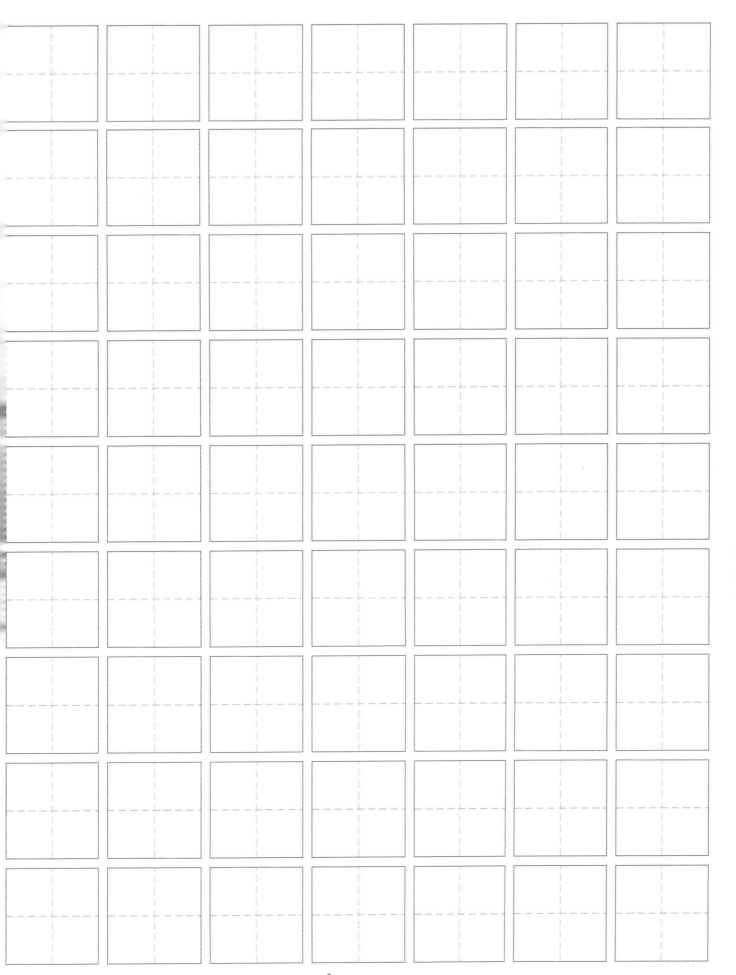

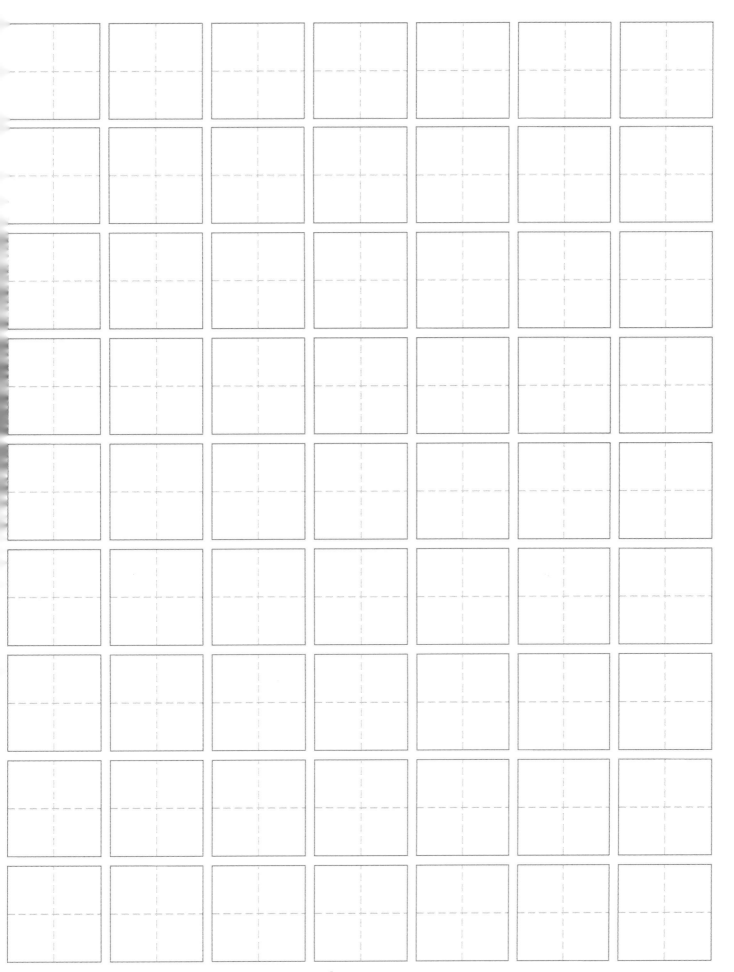

曉機器人

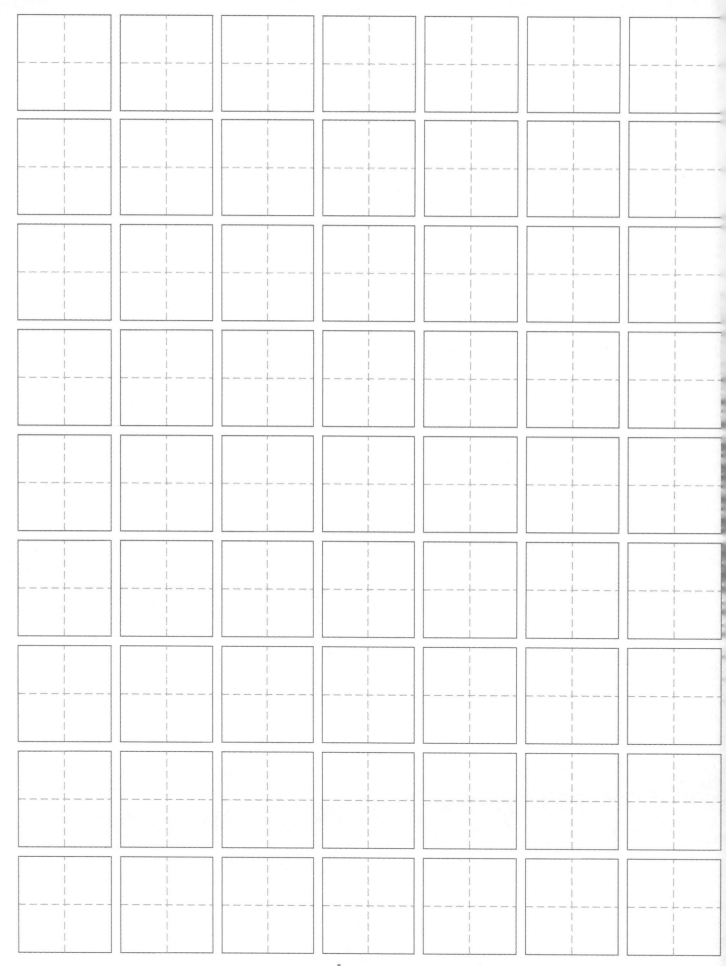

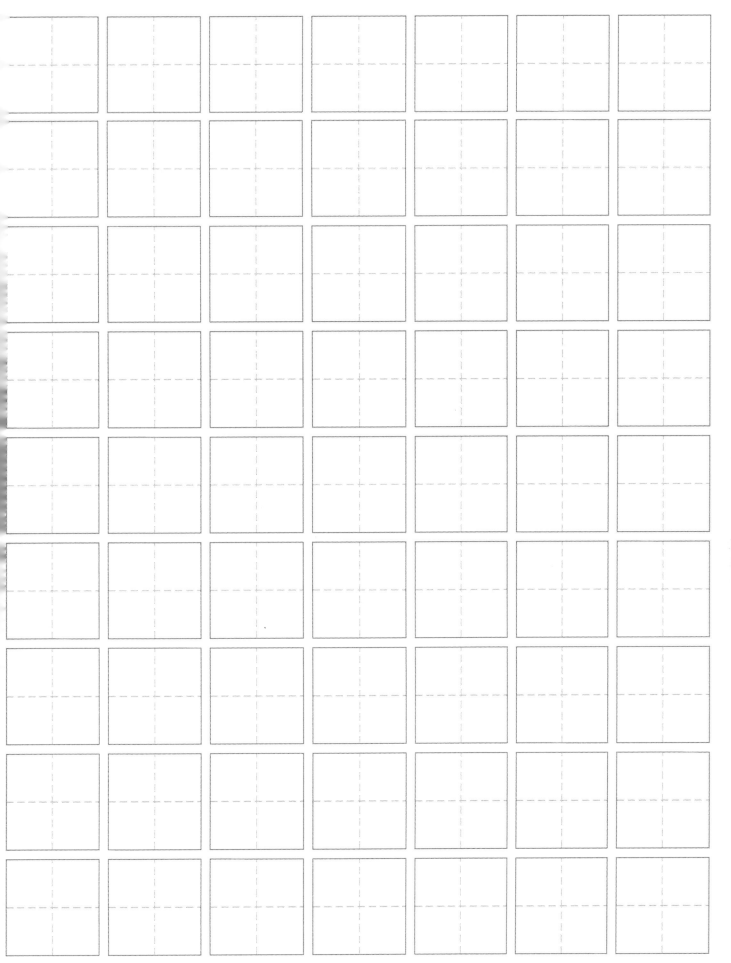

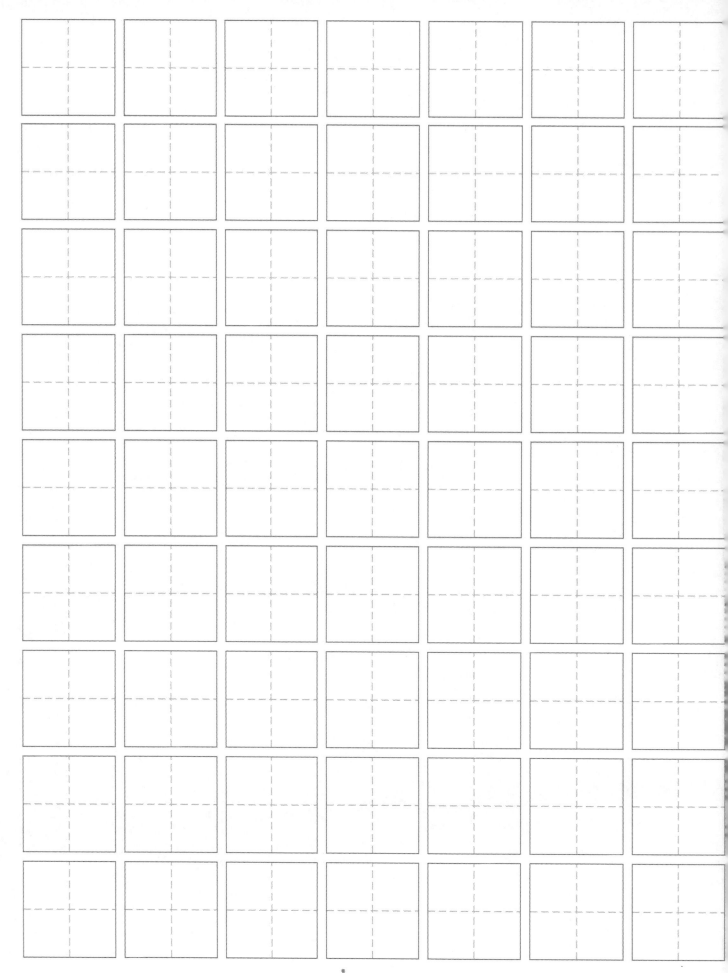

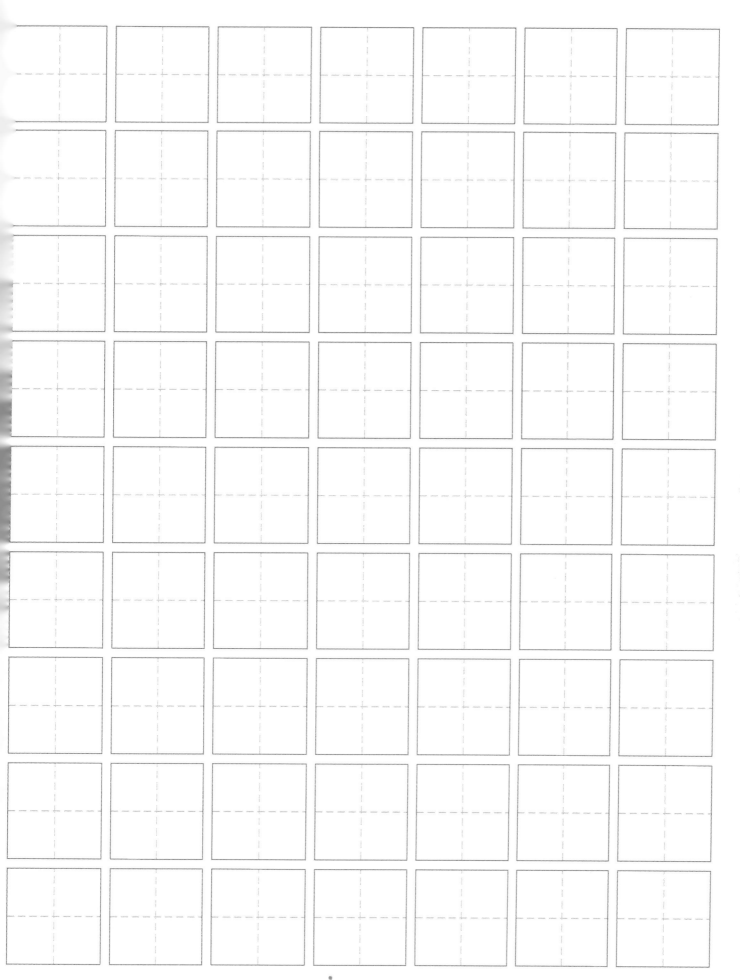

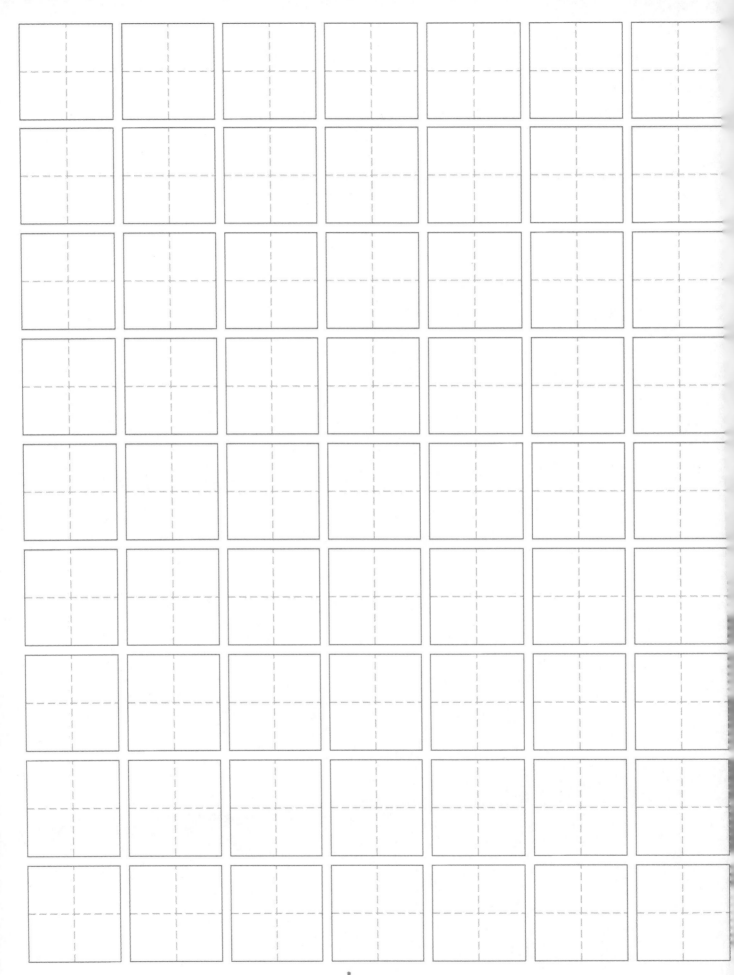

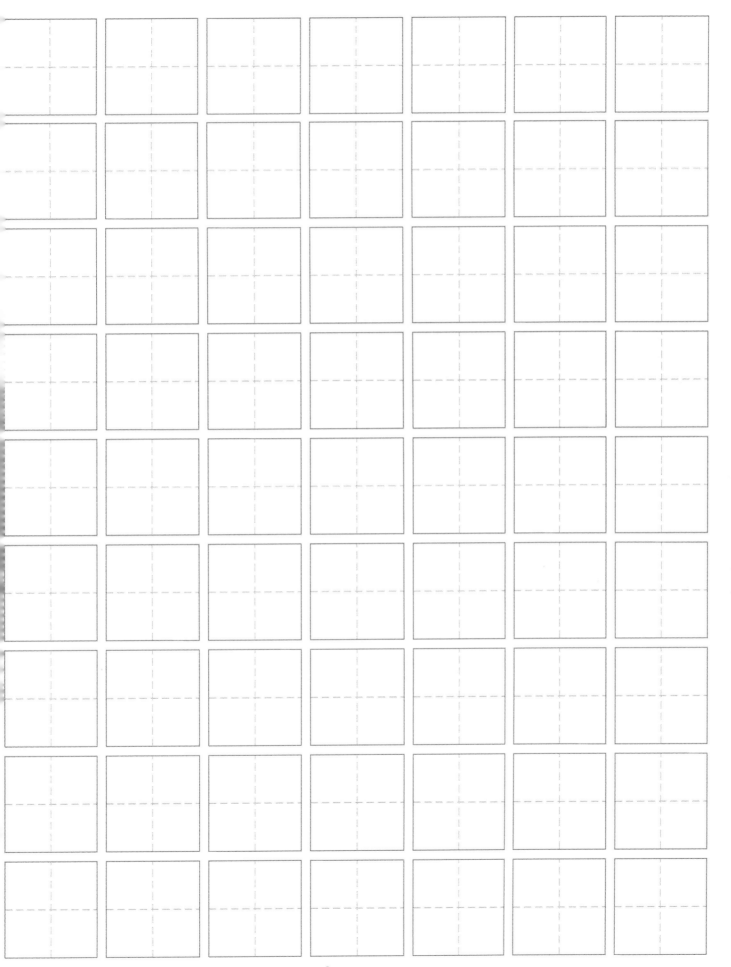

曉機器人

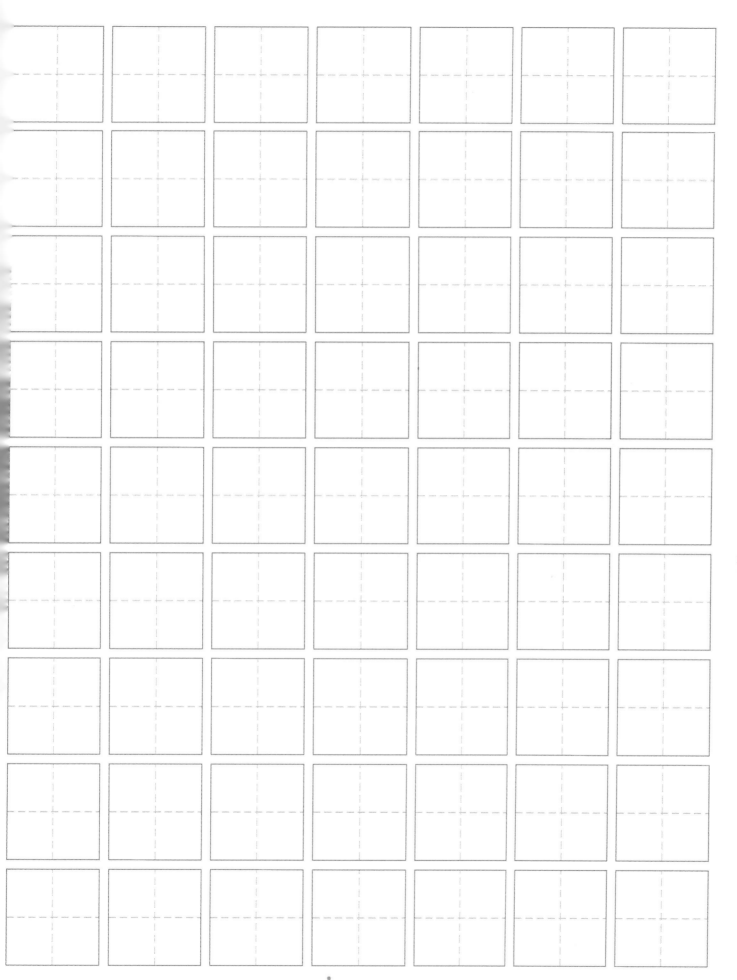

曉機器人

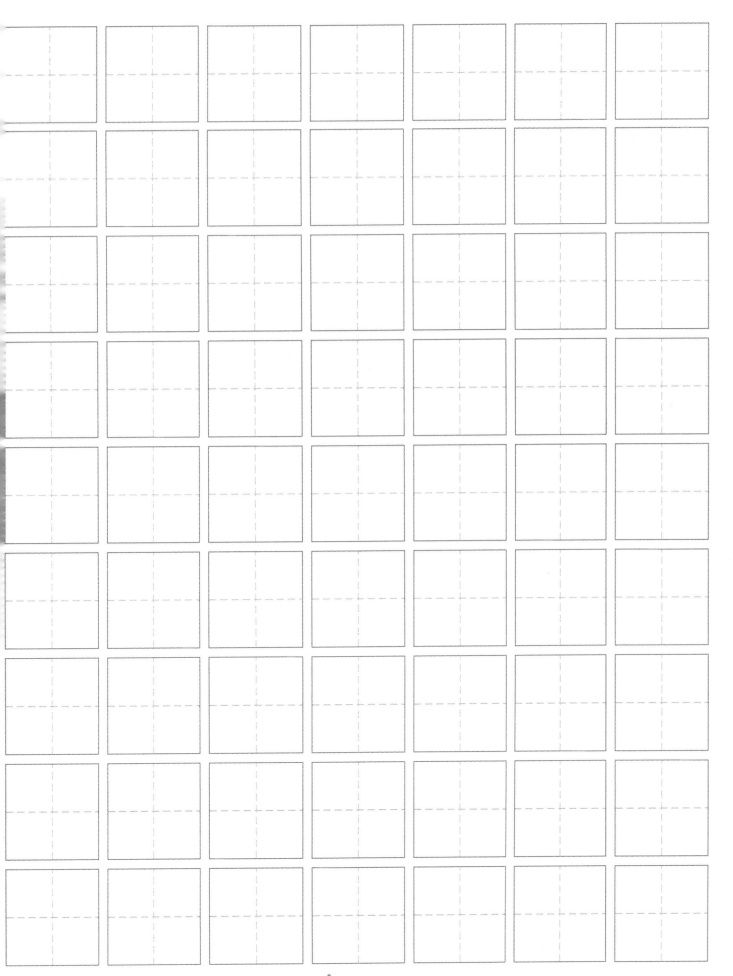

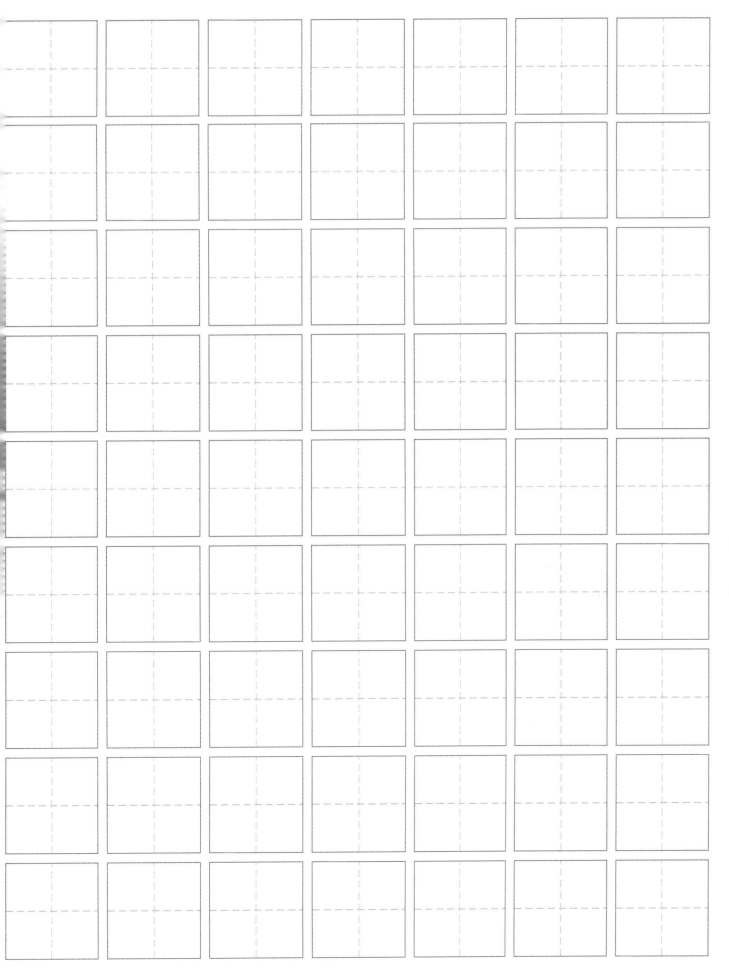

曉機器人

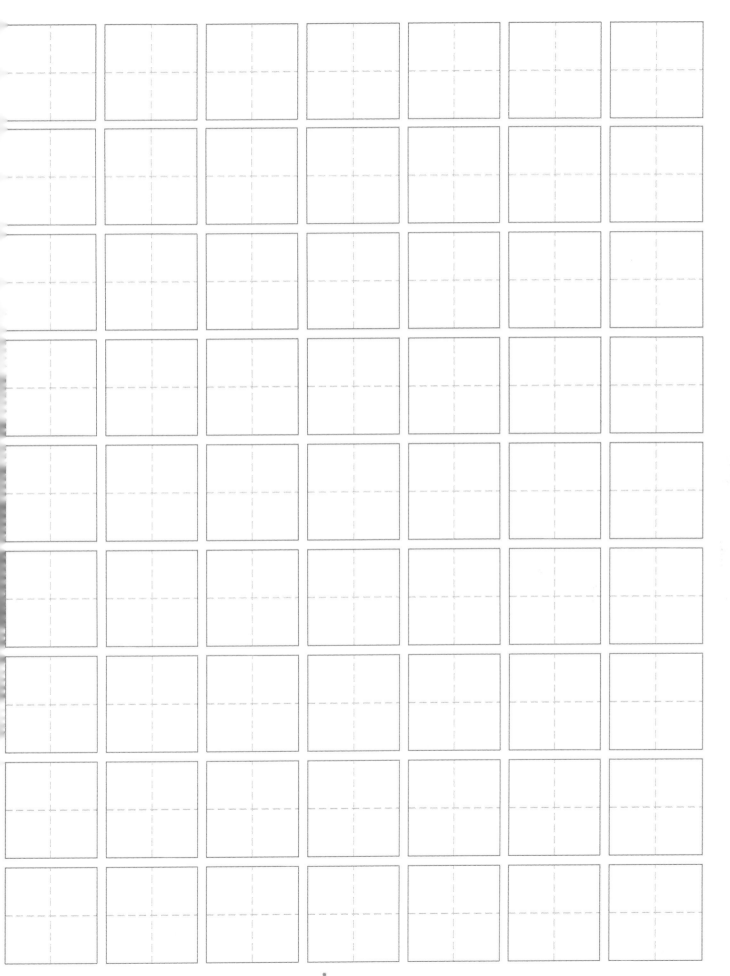

曉機器人

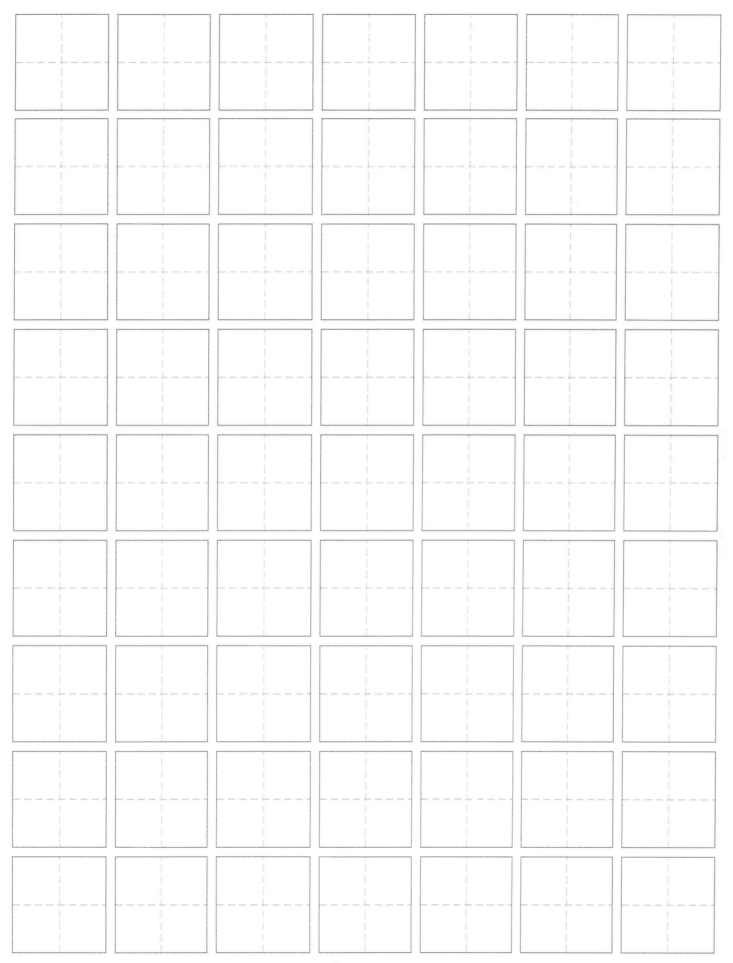

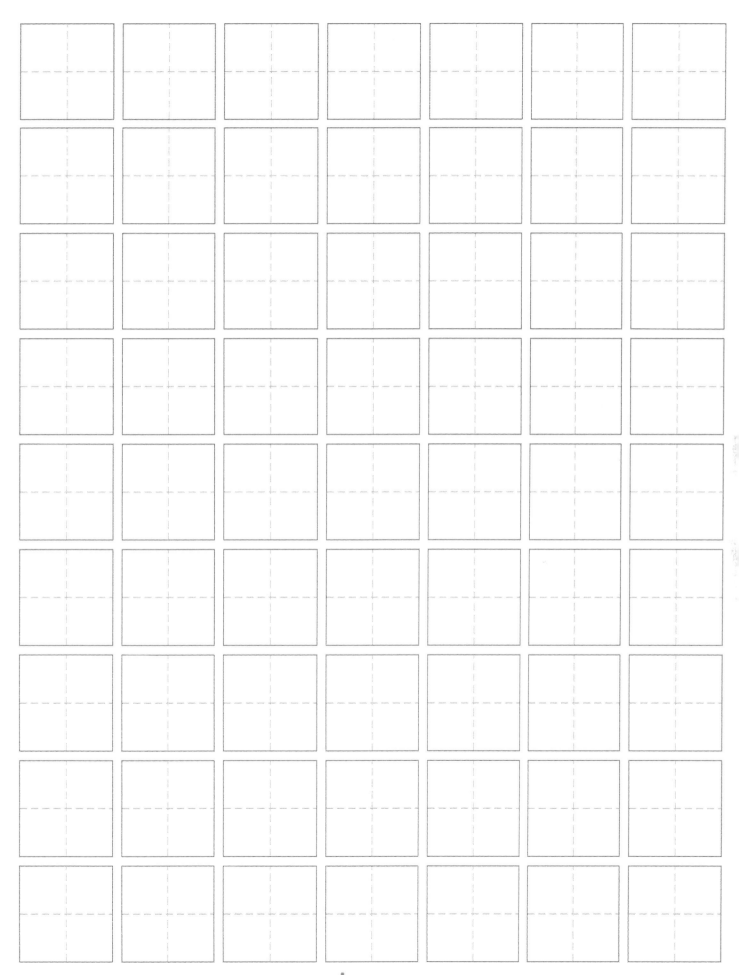

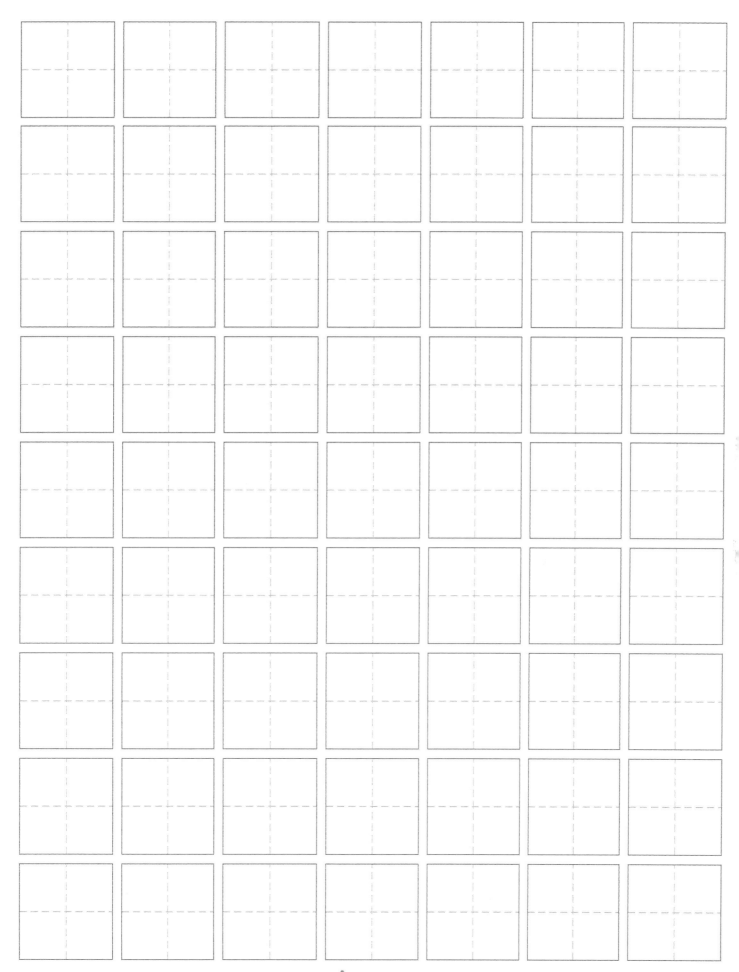

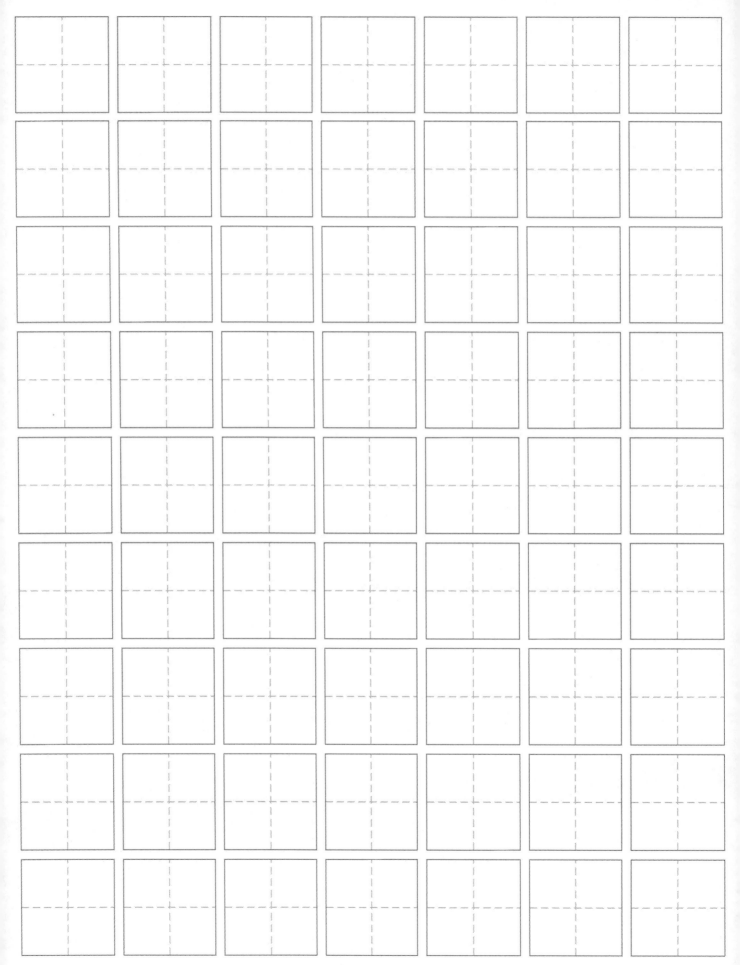

曉機器人

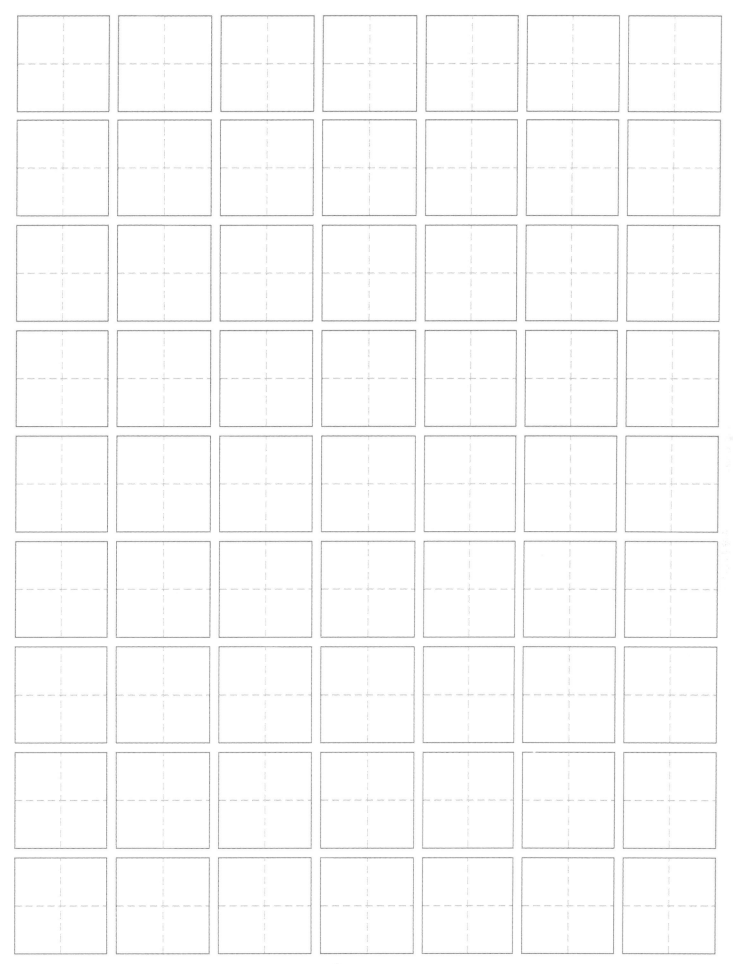

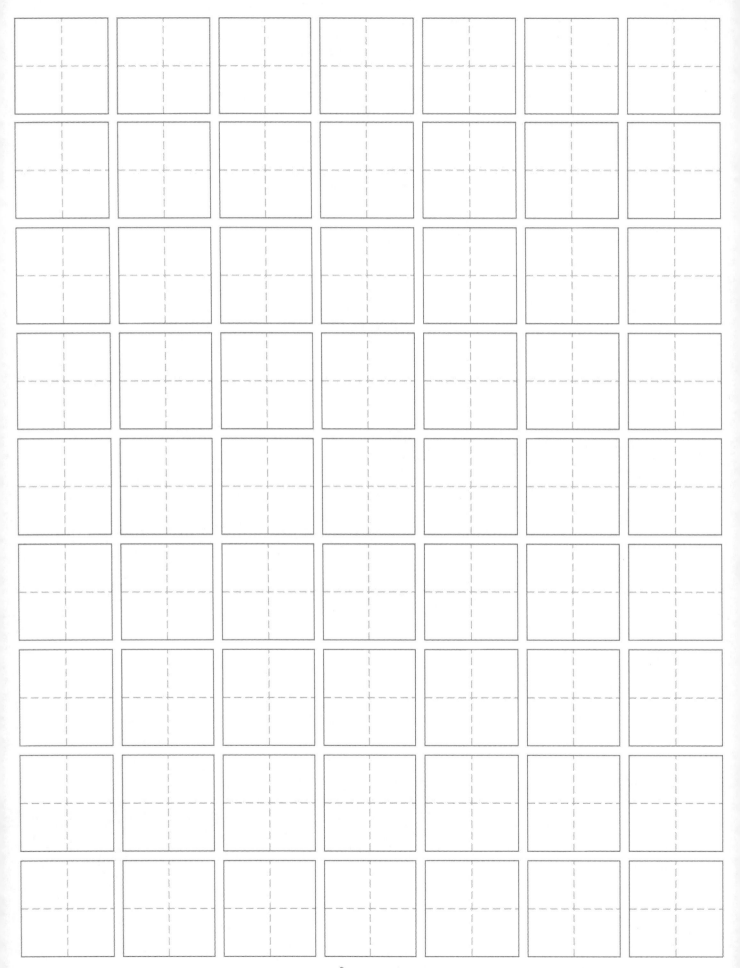

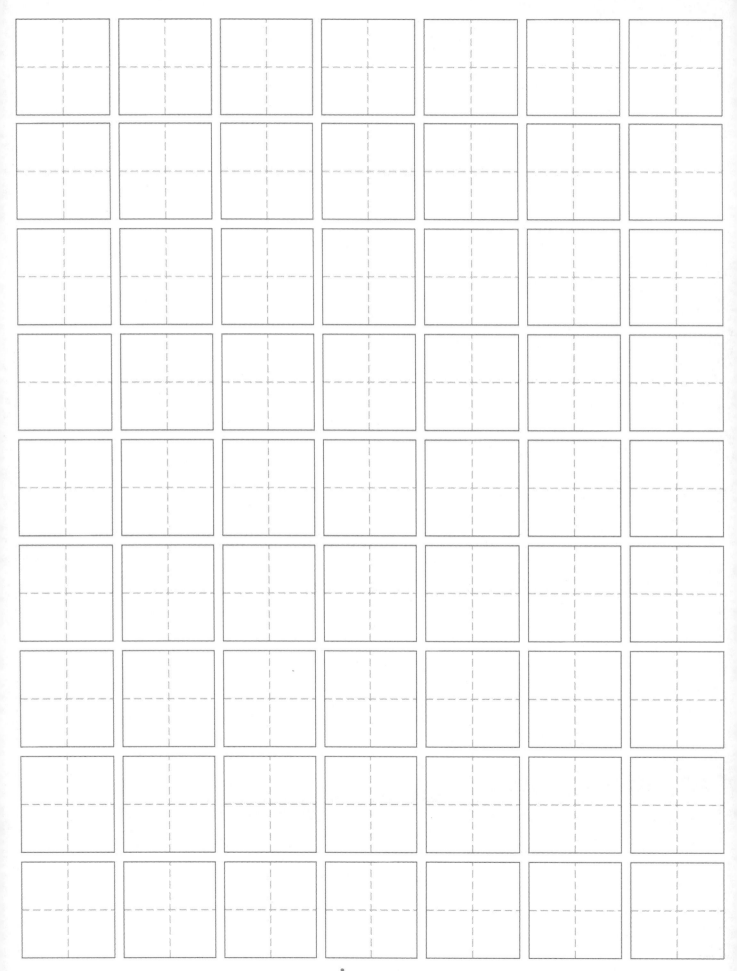

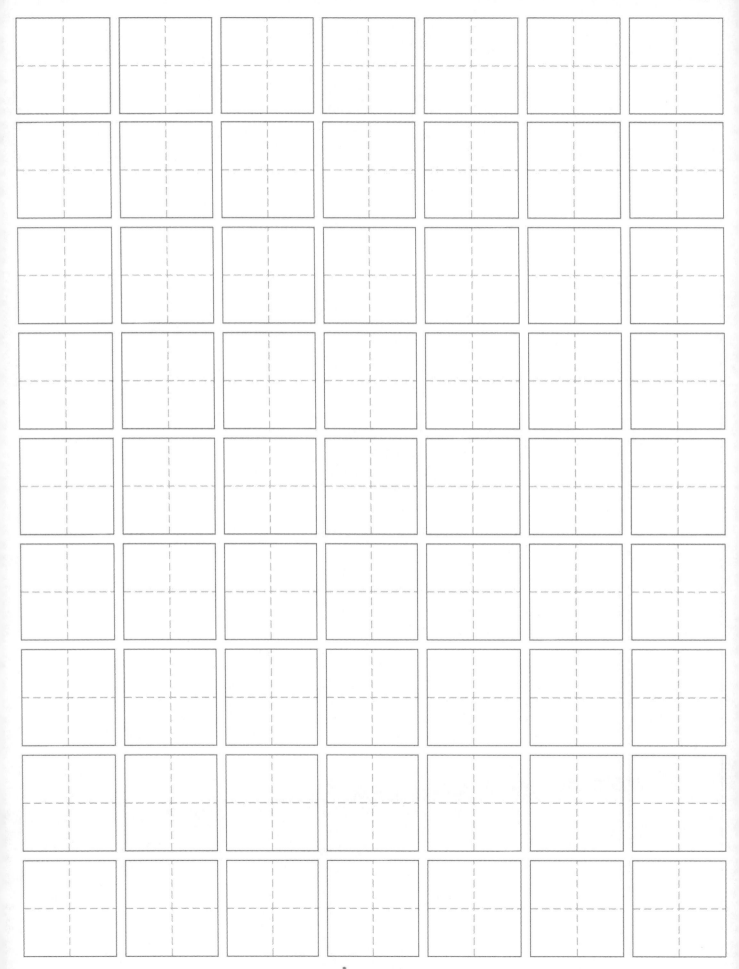

曉機器人

曉機器人

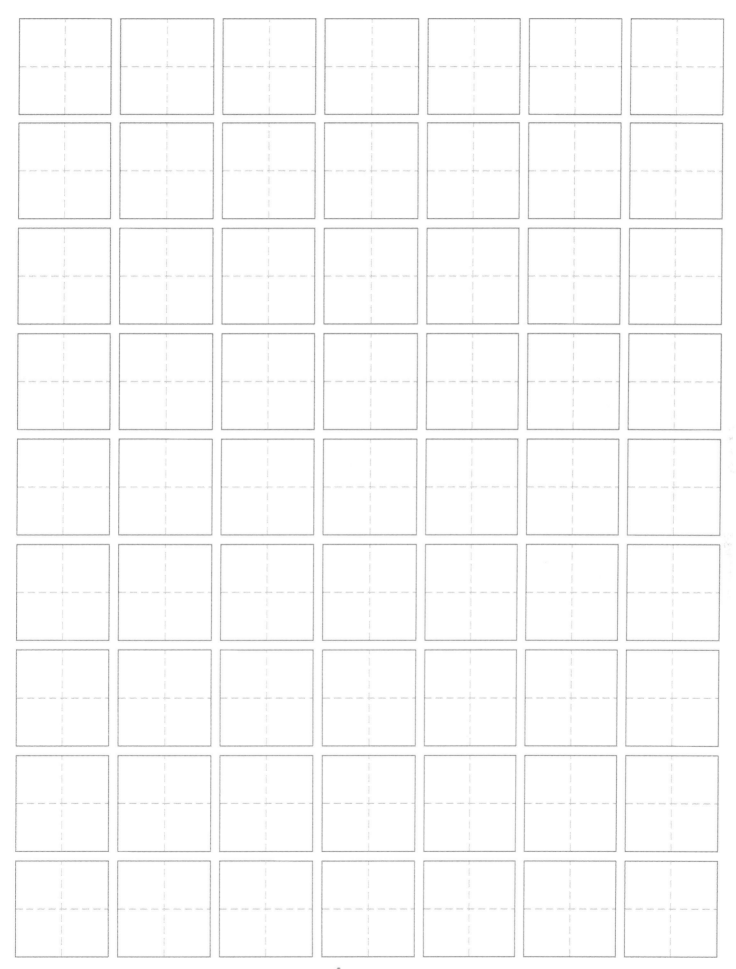

曉機器人

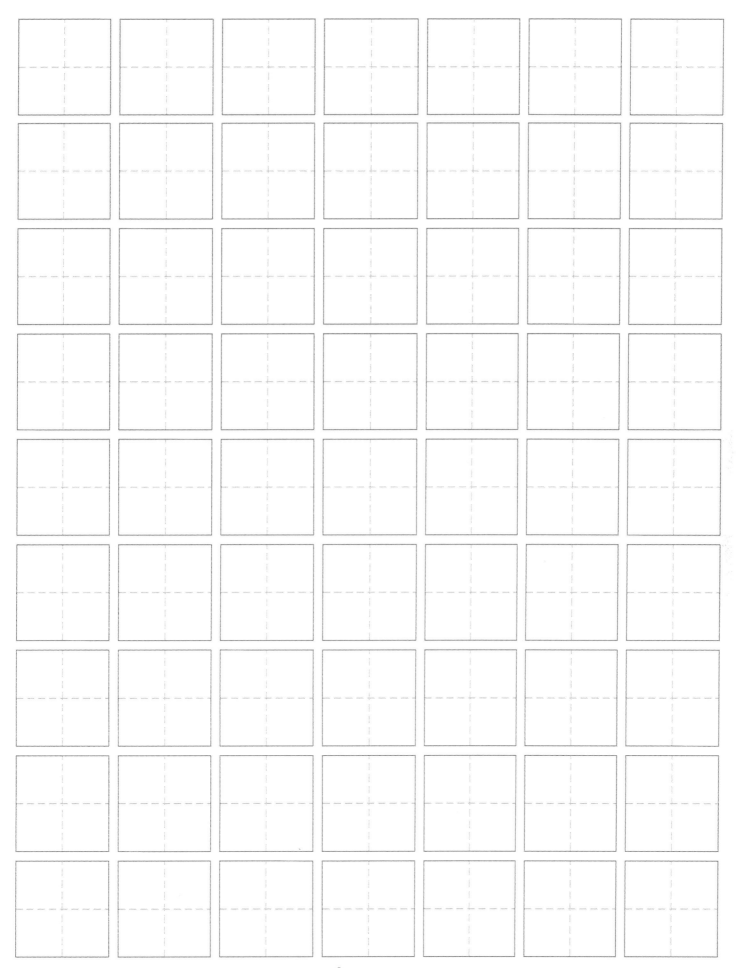

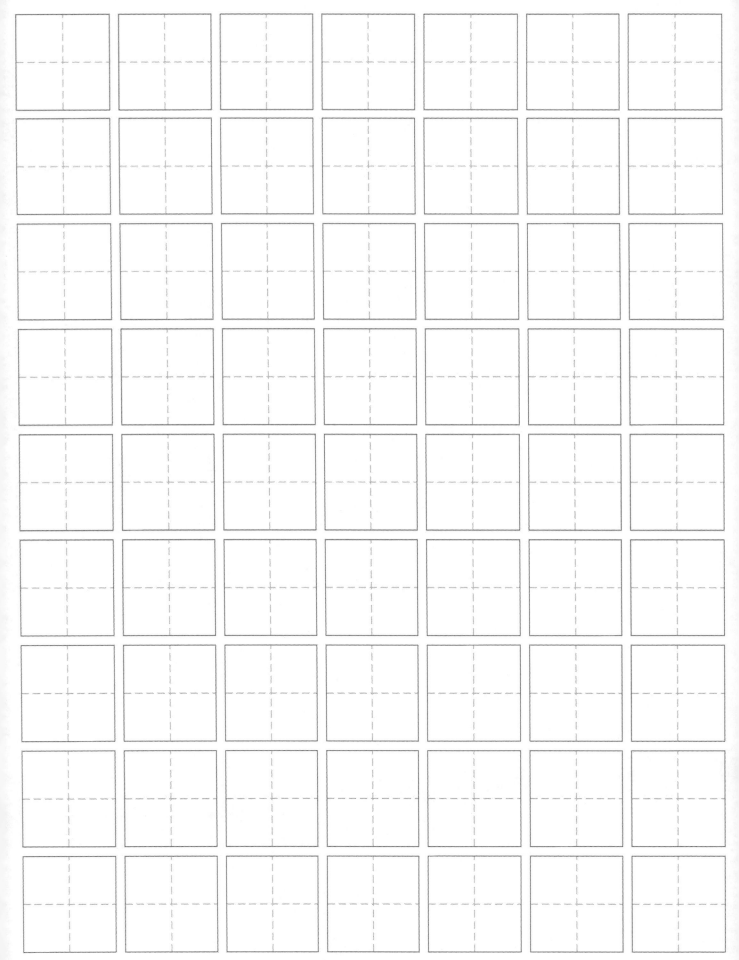

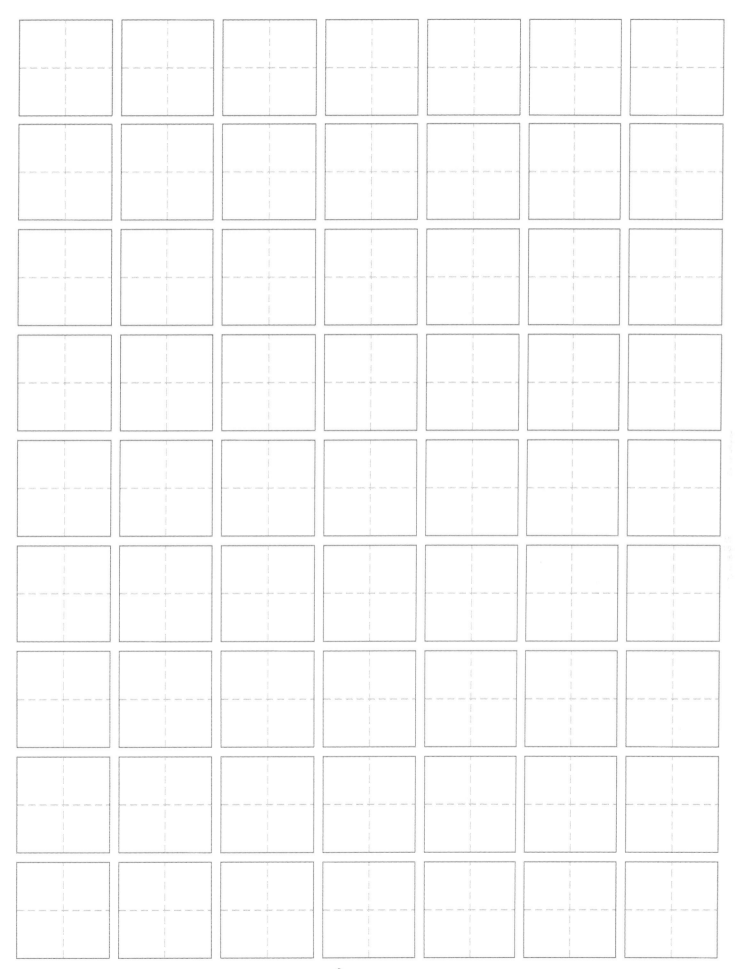